Lita & Jean: Memoirs of Two Generations of Military Women
By Lita Tomas & Jean Marie McNamara
© Copyright 2022 Master Wings Publishing
ISBN: 978-1-64663-013-4
masterwingspublishing.com

MASTER
WINGS
PUBLISHING

LITA & JEAN

Memoirs of Two Generations of Military Women

Lita Tomas & Jean Marie McNamara

MASTER
WINGS
PUBLISHING

DEDICATION:

We would like to thank Col. (IL) Jennifer Pritzker, IL ARNG (Retired) for giving us the opportunity to tell our story, work through our memories of the past, and possibly lay some demons to rest. We are both honored to know you.

Sergeant First Class Raymond Frank Maurer,
may you forever rest in peace.

To our family and friends who have supported us over the years: thank you!

To Sonya, our editor extraordinaire: thank you for molding our thoughts and words into this book.

CONTENTS

LITA

1

LITA: AMBITIONS

I WAS BORN IN 1954, on Chanute Air Force Base in Champaign, Illinois. My parents, Genevieve Wendell and Andrew T. Golabek, might not have been expecting a child. The marriage, I have been told, was not well received by my maternal grandparents, and the relationship ended before I was even born and shortly prior to my biological father's shipping out to the Korean War. The only hints I have about him do not cast him in a positive light.

Despite having been born on an Air Force Base, joining the armed forces was the furthest thing from my mind when I was growing up. With a strong aptitude for science and the desire to be of service to others, I always knew I wanted to help people.

My parents formally divorced soon after my birth, something practically unheard of in the 1950s. Five years later, my mother remarried a Korean War Army veteran one year older than her. John Scaro, the man I would always consider to be my father, started out in my life as a driver of the school van that took me to and from nursery school. As this was prior to the days of safety restraints and child seats, I would stand behind the driver's seat and look out the window, my nose continually dripping on the back of the shirt of this dark-haired Italian college student.

One day, John teasingly complained to my mother that I was ruining his dress shirts before he could go to his classes. She apologized, and took his shirt to the dry cleaners. He left that morning in just his undershirt, and returned at the end of the day to retrieve his clean, pressed shirt and deliver a bouquet of flowers to my mom. From that day forward, he carried a white cotton handkerchief in his back pocket.

Theirs was to be a lifelong and fruitful relationship. My mother would say, "when a Catholic Italian man hung his trousers on the pant-stand next to the bed, another bambino was sure to follow."

I soon found myself the eldest of eight in the tight quarters of a three-bedroom, one bathroom apartment in Chicago. My mother and stepfather had one bedroom, the boys: John, Frank, Mike, and Bob, shared a bedroom, and my three sisters: Linda, Mary, and Geniece, shared the third bedroom. For privacy, I slept on the unheated back porch. The baby of the family cried nonstop and was relegated to the walk-in pantry off the kitchen. As the eldest, I was a deft hand at handwashing all of the laundry, cooking, and cleaning. I could bandage up simple cuts and scrapes before the tears started to roll.

If you lined up all of my siblings, von Trapp style, you would notice a dichotomy of genetics. Five of the seven children, those from my mother's second marriage, inherited my stepfather's olive complexion, average build, and dark brown hair. My brother Mike and sister Geniece were the outliers, with their blond locks and pale complexions. They were all gifted with my mother's artistic talents, and our home was a haven for arts and crafts.

My stepfather, John, formally adopted me, yet I always felt like a bit of an outsider to his large Italian Catholic family. John served along with my godfather in the 866th Transportation Company, Port of Incheon, Korea. My uncle Butch, my mother's only brother, was also in the Army, but served a decade later in Germany.

Military service, however, wasn't regularly discussed at the dinner table. My male relatives had done their tour or two of duty during the war, and then hung up their uniforms and came back to Chicago to work the nine-to-five routine as civilians. My stepfather and godfather were in coffee sales and my uncle Butch worked for the City of Chicago as a union painter and neighborhood committeeman. They were all hardworking individuals who put family first. My mother decided that being a homemaker was vital, especially with eight children living under one roof!

I attended a Catholic grammar school seven out of my first eight years, as did my brothers and sisters, as a Catholic education was important to my stepfather. In school, religion was given the same import as math, reading, and history. Our teachers, all Catholic nuns, used intimidation and physical reprimands to mold our young minds. We were taught to memorize facts and soak up information rather than to think for ourselves. I suppose their abuse could be compared to the harassment that a drill sergeant might hand out during Basic Training. We were taught about the wonder of serving a higher power as a nun, or the moral compass that might guide the boys in my class into the priesthood. Certainly, the nuns did not mention serving in the armed forces.

We were supportive of our nation, don't get me wrong. At least, we said the Pledge of Allegiance regularly, but aside from weekly bomb-raid drills that had us hiding under our desks, service to our country and civic duty were foreign concepts.

Speaking of foreign, as this was before 1964, those were the days of Latin Mass, so while I did understand that a world with cultures and languages other than my American English existed, it took me another dozen or so years to put two and two together and realize that Ave Maria was actually the Hail Mary in song.

As an eighth grader, the career path I saw for myself had

a religious slant. The sisters of Notre Dame de Namur had the honorable task of leading and training young minds in our parish in Chicago, and they inspired me. Educators both inside and outside of the classroom, they ensured that we had a solid foundation in the Catholic Church and the basics of education to succeed in the high schools of our choosing. A career for the female members of Catholic-Italian families was pretty simple: young women were groomed to be good housewives and mothers or to join the sisters in teaching or nursing. So unsurprisingly, I thought I would be a mother or a nun. By this time, I had four brothers: the youngest, Bob (Robert), a few weeks old, was named after my Uncle Butch. He would be the last Scaro, and would round out our numbers, making it four girls and four boys.

I guess I could have considered camp counseling, as it seemed my life revolved around creating crafts or other activities to keep my siblings occupied. Women were not even allowed to join the Army at that time. If a woman wanted to support the military she would have to join the Women's Army Corps or Women's Auxiliary Corps (WAC).

The paths I followed until I did join were not what I expected or desired. They were difficult, unsatisfactory, and cruel, and yet I survived. In many ways, I have always been at war. I am battle scarred from life.

2
LITA: PRE-ARMY YEARS

DURING THE TRANSITION FROM EIGHTH grade to high school, I realized for the first time that the world could change on a dime. The first eight years of my education had been very structured. I even wore a uniform: a simple pleated skirt no shorter than mid-kneecap, a white blouse, and a vest. Neither the schedule nor the teachers changed. There were never any conflicts among my peers or the staff.

The teachers and staff of my elementary school—nuns, of course—were a mysterious breed, shrouded in their habits, long black wool robes that draped to the floor. Their heads and necks were covered with black veils. Starched crisp white collars covered their hair, making them appear to be floating, disembodied faces. Once, when I was in second or third grade, and these looming black hulks floated behind me as I cowered at my desk, I did wonder if they were actually humans, rather than divine incarnations.

Looking back, I wonder how the nuns wielded such power. They never raised their voices. Occasionally, they would raise a ruler and whack our knuckles, but the only item they used to gain the attention of the class was their "clicker," a wooden handheld device they activated by thumb pressure. When triggered, a loud wooden *click* sounded as one wooden lever sprang forth to strike the handle. That effective trick kept the class in order, much like an animal trainer keeps a dog in line.

After the rather uneventful yet formative years of Catholic grammar school, I graduated with a class of only about forty peers. I was shocked and awed as I entered a suburban public high school district that numbered over a thousand for each class level! The noise difference alone was disturbing. Where I had once walked the school halls in silence—considered an easier way to reach God—I now found myself immersed in an alien adventure, with hundreds of students chatting and rushing from one class to the next. There was no order. There was only chaos!

Home wasn't peaceful either. For example: I had gone to sleep away camp the summer before high school, and returned to find out from a neighbor that my family had moved. No one had mentioned that we might be moving. No one was there to meet me when I returned from camp. I was alone and terrified.

Later that day my aunt, Mary, my mother's sister, picked me up, and we drove out to our new home in the Oak Park suburb of Chicago. I was awed that so much had changed while I was away, and that I had no control over these changes.

My new public high school was a huge monolith of a building. The curriculum intimidated me, too. Administrators offered us dozens of class choices, including history, math, English, social science, language arts, physical science, and physical fitness. We could also wear whatever we wanted. Girls could even wear pants! No uniforms!

The class sizes at my new school might have been easier for the students transferring in from other suburban public schools to adapt to. But as a student transferring from a private Catholic school, I found the transition difficult at best. I was now a fish in what felt like a very large pond.

To survive, I needed extra help in a few classes. I gladly stayed after school or showed up early to get help from teachers who actually talked to me like a human being. I loved that these educators were approachable.

The other reason I chose to go to school early was that I had developed into a very early riser. While our new home had more bedrooms, and I now had one to myself, we still shared one bathroom. When you share a bathroom with nine other people, it's best to get in and out first. This might have been a helpful habit later when I served in the armed services, too. They do get up early!

I didn't make friends easily in the first year. I immersed myself in my coursework to avoid feeling out of place. I immediately found two teachers and my dean to be a source of refuge. My algebra teacher, Alex Moerle, in particular took pride in his personal collection of live plants that lined the windowsills of his classroom. I volunteered to help with their maintenance, watering, pruning, and transplanting when necessary. I had always loved nature and had often camped and fished, but I had never had any pets except snails, which I raised along with my tropical fish in a small aquarium in my bedroom. Snails are quite easy to raise, so I ended up with hundreds, which I sold to neighbors. They became my signature. To signal to my teacher that I had finished watering his plants, I'd draw a snail on his blackboard.

Seeing schoolwork as a refuge, I often asked for extra assignments to do outside of school. On Saturday nights, I went back to my Catholic roots by volunteering to play guitar at our new local church. There, I partnered with three other high schoolers: a female singer and two male guitarists. Two adults sponsored us: one a grandfatherly vocal arranger, and the other a recent graduate from the local Seminary. The priest, appointed to his position at age twenty eight, was an electronic hobbyist.

He managed the mikes and mixed the voices and equipment for a better tone during mass. We first met when I was fourteen or fifteen years old. He would often invite our small group out for pizza, invitations we accepted to varying degrees.

During my senior year at Oak Park and River Forest High School, our group decided to enter a church variety show that would take place in the basement of the Catholic grammar school next to our church. We practiced for several weeks to prepare ourselves to sing in front of our family, friends, and neighbors.

The evening of the show, we wrapped up late. I was seventeen. It was a Friday night, and after packing up equipment and saying our goodbyes, Father Pete asked me if I could help him carry his equipment to the rectory, the small building adjacent to the church where a priest usually lives. I obliged, good little Catholic girl that I was, and we each took handfuls of electronic wires and cables next door. Once I dumped the cables inside, I turned to depart, but Father Pete asked if I would like a cup of coffee. I never turned down a cup of coffee—my dad was a coffee salesman, so the beverage flowed through my veins like blood. I took a cup and we sat quietly in Father Pete's large living room. The coffee was unusually sweet and chocolatey. This was a taste I couldn't put my finger on, not unpleasant, but certainly not like my typical cup of joe.

I awoke the next morning in a bed I didn't recognize, without clothes, and without a memory of what had happened the night before. I found my clothes on the floor, quickly dressed, and walked out of the bedroom in search of answers. The other side of the door was Father Pete's sitting room, but he was not there, so I quickly grabbed my guitar and rushed out of the rectory.

When I arrived home, my mother was furious. I had not called home, she didn't know where I had been, and I was probably grounded. I went to my room and tried to make sense of the night before. I don't sleep without clothes. I don't sleep at other people's homes; I certainly don't sleep at rectories! What had happened?

That night at mass, Father Pete was very quiet. He didn't talk to any of us as we set up and played his service. Once we were finished, I asked my friend what she thought about my account of the previous night's events. She took me to her house and told her mother, who called my mother, and by the time I got home, I entered a hostile environment I didn't recognize.

I was told I was a sinner. I had tempted a priest. I was this, and I was that. I was also grounded for the rest of the school year. I couldn't leave my room unless it was to eat or do dishes or go to class. I tolerated my punishment, feeling like maybe I was at fault. But why couldn't I remember what had happened?

A month passed without incident, but then, as May arrived, I discovered that I had missed a period. I was as regular as clockwork. Was it possible that I had been raped by a priest, and that I was pregnant? I put these thoughts out of my mind and kept to my studies.

I had been a happy, content person before that night. In my last year of high school, my signature changed. It evolved from the lowly snail to "Live, Love, Laugh!" or "LLL!" if I was in a hurry. Now, however, my "LLL!" signature and smile felt forced. The normal joy I had once found in life was replaced by a fear I couldn't face. I gathered the courage to tell my mother that I had missed my period, and she immediately took me to our doctor. It wasn't 100% certain, but it appeared I was indeed pregnant.

My parents were beyond inconsolable. They went to the church and filed a complaint. Father Pete was told to leave the Rectory and await a decision by the Cardinal. They kept things quiet. I made the decision that if I was with child, I would keep the baby, like a good little Catholic girl. Pete, no longer a 'Father' but soon to become a biological father, decided that he would provide for us both to try and make things right. Appearances! That was all he was doing, making a token expression. This wouldn't be a union of love! He and I never discussed how I felt through all of this. I retreated into my mind.

Life, I found, can change on a dime, and mine was a whirlwind of activity for the next six weeks.

For graduation, my hair was done, and I wore a white dress. The next day, I got married in that same dress with that same two-foot high hairdo with forty bobby pins holding it together, so popular in the late '70s. We had a civil union at the courthouse in Chicago, Illinois. I did not want this marriage, but there was the stigma of being an unwed mother, and pressure from my parents overwhelmed me. I tried and failed to climb out the window of the courthouse bathroom. The small square pane was sealed closed by dozens of years of paint. I wanted to run away. I wanted to start over.

The next day, we both put our personal belongings in Pete's car and moved to an apartment in Lincoln Park, Michigan. Pete had gotten a job at an electronics store, and I sat in an empty apartment with scarce furnishings, alone and afraid, far from family and friends.

In mid-July, I was rushed to the hospital with terrible cramping, and found I had miscarried my first child.

No longer being pregnant made me more at ease, but I was still married. My parents had raised me to believe marriage is a sacred bond. At age eighteen, I had ended up married to this man, and I would continue to be married to him even if it had a horrible beginning.

Soon, I wound up pregnant again, and again miscarried the child.

A year passed, and I was pregnant for a third time, but this time I carried the child to term, and delivered a healthy baby girl, Jean Marie McNamara, on May 17, 1974. By this time, my husband and I had moved back to the Chicago area, and my stepfather had had a change of heart, accepting my daughter and me into the family.

Although I had helped extensively with my siblings, having your own child is something that equates to nothing else! This beautiful happy baby that I was able to nurse and care for was the miracle I never expected in my life, and yet here she was.

Pete didn't seem to have the same feelings about bringing a child into the world. He grew quieter and spent more time at work, drinking or smoking away his inner frustrations. My stepfather, however, loved his granddaughter with every ounce of his being. He insisted we come over often so he could hold her and play with her tiny toes as she slept in his arms.

Almost immediately after that, my second daughter was born. Kymberly (Kym) Ann McNamara joined our family on September 12, 1975. She was a beautiful, blond-haired, blue-eyed little girl whom I found a bit easier to care for after her older sister Jean Marie showed me the ropes.

When Kym was about two months old, I woke up early one morning to the sound of her screaming at the top of her lungs. I ran to her crib, expecting to see a diaper pin opened and penetrating her hip. I quickly assessed the diaper and found both pins still latched securely, so I lifted her up to hold her. I could tell immediately that there was something terribly wrong. She was burning up. I didn't need a thermometer to tell me that she had a very high fever.

I immediately called our pediatrician, bundled Kym and Jean up, and drove directly to the next suburb of Forest Park where the pediatrician had her office. The doctor took Kym's temperature and performed a rather quick exam as Jean played with toys on the floor of the waiting room.

I was instructed to take Kym to McNeal Hospital in Berwyn post-haste. As I drove, my mind spun, *what was wrong?*

The doctor wasn't positive, but she suspected that my tiny baby girl had meningitis. And she was correct. The horror of the next few days were nearly unbearable. I was allowed to stay in the room with her and watch her, and hope beyond dire predictions that the doctors were telling me.

I prayed over her for healing even as the priest administered the "Anointing of the Sick," then called "Last Rites." I watched helplessly as she lay on an ice mattress to try and bring her fever down. After three days, her fever finally broke. After two more days, we were allowed to return home. Home, to my husband.

No one ever liked the husband. He was physically abusive when he drank, and he drank a lot. He appeared to have numbed all senses but one, his explosive anger, which I was forced to live with for the remainder of my marriage. Three to four days a week, a drunk, angry man lived in our home. Again, I felt the strong Catholic tenets of family, so I withstood the hard times.

When my girls turned one and two, however, things changed. I was cleaning the house one day while Pete was at work. Under his recliner chair in the living room, I found something that beyond turned my stomach: three magazines depicting grown men engaging in various types of sexual activities with children ranging from girls in school uniforms to young toddlers. I took my baby daughters, left the apartment, and went back to my parents' house, shaking with anger.

Decades later, I was horrified to learn that the Archdiocese of Chicago pursued internal rumors that pedophile magazines were found in Pete's dwelling during seminary. Pete was delayed a year and did not graduate with his class; the investigation suggested that his horrific interest -- "bizarre behavior," as the 2014 Archdiocese released internal documents detail-- was the reason for this. Of course, it was just a slight delay. But there was no accountability, and no corrective action. He was still permitted to become a priest, and they put him in my family's parish and allowed him to supervise teenagers and young children.

Some lines cannot be crossed, and he crossed one. I was no longer the obedient good little Catholic girl; I was first and foremost a good mother.

To survive on my own, I took two jobs. My mother watched the girls while I was at work. This was probably the hardest part of my life. Realizing that such a thing could happen to my daughters, and that my ignorance had placed both of them in danger, made me red with rage. I developed a temper I never thought I could hold in a heart full of empathy for all mankind. I decided that whatever it took, I would keep my daughters safe. This was a promise I almost couldn't keep, however. Divorce and custody battles are very, very expensive and convoluted.

3
LITA: FIRST AID FOR TANKS?

WHAT I REALLY NEEDED WAS a career. I started with a list of my strengths and weaknesses to help guide me in the right direction. I had loved the science classes I had taken in high school, including Advanced Placement Biology, Chemistry, and Physics, and had volunteered in the biology lab as an assistant to the department chair. I had lived for biology.

In my high school, I had conducted pond research that examined microscopic organisms in local ponds. I grew slime mold and re-plated microscope slides that had yellowed with age, so that future classes could use them in their educational pursuits. Life cycle studies were taken to another extreme as I hatched duck eggs and taught the new hatchlings to follow me up and down the first-floor halls of our school's science department. The education was excellent, but would I be suited for a career in science?

To get a job I both wanted and believed would make enough money to raise my children on my own, I was told I needed a college degree. My top choice for a career was in the medical field. I had a propensity for everything scientific. I felt nurturing deep in my soul and I believed that if I could aim high, I could pursue nursing, and possibly teach medicine afterwards.

Being an optimist has always allowed me to push further than my peers, and this was the time to act! Researching education costs at local colleges and universities quickly quelled my optimism, however. Working at a minimum wage job while attending school would not be the best choice for my family for the next four to six years.

Animals, by nature, hunt or gather food, protect their young from predators, or find shelter for rest. Once restricted or caged, the animal endures stress, which can cause mental, physical, and behavioral problems. Before you wonder if I somehow mixed in a different genre of book, fear not! As members of the animal kingdom, humans can feel caged or restrained in the face of negative emotional pressure, which, like when other animals are caged, can lead to stress. This is what I experienced.

Previously, I felt trapped by an abusive husband and a religion that had let me down. I had escaped that cage, but was about to enter another. I was now a single mother with few opportunities to create a nurturing environment for my children. Without financial stability or a career, I didn't know how I would put food on the table or a roof over our heads. Stress was high! I urgently needed a solution, some way of keeping my long-term plan while living comfortably in the interim. Well, maybe not comfortably, but at least with less stress.

My divorce was pending, and even that didn't go as I had hoped. Since no one in our family would admit to ever being divorced and no one in my circle of friends had ever been divorced, choosing an attorney was difficult. I looked through the Yellow Pages and picked a man in a small office on the near north side of Chicago. I brought him the evidence: the magazines I had found. His response floored me! I could get a divorce, but could not use the magazines in court to stop visitation, which was a father's right unless there was proof of abuse. These magazines were not enough proof.

I was working at two jobs and hardly seeing my girls, who spent a great deal of time at my parents' home a few blocks away. I worked in retail at a local mall, going from one store to another at midday to give me enough money to pay the rent and buy food, but not much else.

One afternoon, while walking through the mall between jobs, I passed a military recruiter at a small standalone booth. He hailed me over to talk, and I reluctantly stopped to hear what he had to offer. But he didn't have to say a word. Immediately, my eyes spotted the poster standing against the table. It read: "Free College!" I was hooked!

I made an appointment to meet the recruiter at his office in the city the next week. I took the day off work, and without mentioning it to anyone, I grabbed the elevated rail downtown.

Chicago has a unique public transportation system that winds through the local neighborhoods and culminates in a circle around the downtown area. The commuter trains are at ground level as they start out in the farthest reaches of the city neighborhoods, but they rise above ground to form an elevated system once they enter the city. This elevated track network is affectionately known as "the L." There is also a segment that shoots underground in a subway, and buses and taxis roam the main streets, so you can easily navigate the city.

Upon arriving at the recruiting office, I noticed a bank of offices on both sides of the hallway as I walked along. First there was the Marines, and then across the hall from that was a small lounge with a vending machine and a coffee pot. A little further down the hall, the Coast Guard and Navy had staked out spots. At the end of the hallway, across from each other, I finally approached the last two offices—the U.S. Army and Air Force. The Air Force office—bingo! I had arrived.

As soon as the Air Force recruiter spotted me at the door, he jumped up and rushed over to greet me. *My, this is a gentleman,* I thought, but then he shuffled me back into the hall and we walked briskly until he stopped in front of a large conference room full of people, whom I could see through a glass door. He pushed two number 2 pencils into my hand, gave my name to a Marine at the front of the packed room, and just as abruptly said good luck and left me as he closed the door behind him.

Startled? Shocked? Embarrassed? Confused, for sure! I asked the Marine what exactly was going on, acutely aware of forty or more sets of eyes on me. He said flatly that I needed to take a test to see what position I qualified for. He glanced down at my hand grasping the number 2s tightly in a fist that could have broken under the white-knuckle strain. I eased up somewhat and replied, "Oh, OK" and took the only seat available, in the center of the front row, right in front of the Marine's desk.

A large, sealed white envelope with numbers printed across the top sat on my desk. It contained the Armed Services Vocational Aptitude Battery, or ASVAB. In 1976, when I took it, it was the first implementation of the exam by all of the armed services for selection and classification of new recruits.

Since 1976, a variety of content changes have been introduced to the test. Its overall purpose has remained constant throughout the history of this type of placement testing in the armed services, matching the abilities of recruits to the needs of the service.

When I took the exam, ten subsets made up the overall test. Each subset was designed to reveal an individual's strengths or weaknesses. At the time of my testing, the subsets were Word Knowledge, Arithmetic Reasoning, Mechanical Comprehension, Shop Information, Automobile Information, Electronics Information, Mathematics Knowledge, Numerical Operations, General Science, and General Information.

I tackled a hundred multiple-choice questions, using my pencils to darken the circles for my answer choices on a slim sheet of cardstock. I believe choices A-D were the only options for answers. At the end of the timed test, I brought my packet to the Marine, returned to my seat, and remained quiet as others continued to take the exam. Last one in, first one out. It had been at least an hour, and I was pleased to have finished, but frustrated that I was required to sit quietly and wait for the others to finish, too.

While I sat there, a burly man in uniform reviewed my response sheet. With time on my hands, I noticed that his uniform was stretching at the seams from his muscled frame. *Hmm*, I mused, *men in uniform could be a secondary benefit of joining the service*. I was about to be single.

Suddenly, the man shook me out of my fantasy as he pushed his way out from behind the desk, making his chair screech. He held my answer sheet as he took a step toward the glass paneled door. A few other heads glanced up but then returned to their packets. The man stood halfway out the door, his eyes moving from the hall to the room full of applicants and back to the hall. Finally, he got the attention of another recruiter, and they quickly exchanged comments. Then he returned to his post at the front of the room.

I noticed that the man no longer held my answer sheet. I assumed he had turned it in for processing, and was somewhat relieved my part was over. Soon, I could get on with the rest of my appointment and finally discuss my options with the Air Force recruiter.

A few minutes passed, and the other man who had taken my score sheet returned to the door with a different person, possibly from the Navy or Coast Guard. As they stood outside the glass door, the first man pointed at me and said a few words, to which the man in white dress uniform shook his head. With that, the two left.

What did I do? I wondered. *Did I make a complete disaster of the test? I did finish rather quickly. Maybe I should have double-checked my work?* A bead of sweat had formed on my forehead and was trickling down near my eye. I brushed it away, and thought, *Well, maybe I can take it over next week or next month. There was a lot of math on the test, and I absolutely despise math. Maybe I could practice some at home and just ask to take it again?*

Then I got angry. *No one had even told me there would be a test! This is not my fault! I didn't prepare! I didn't study! I should have been given some kind of warning!* As I was feeling sorry for myself and deciding I should force whoever was in charge to give me another chance, yet another recruiter appeared in the doorway. It was my Air Force recruiter with another Air Force person in a fancier uniform with extra ribbons and medals on his shirt.

My recruiter now pointed at me and must have been explaining that I was his applicant. Then the heavily medaled man nodded once and patted him on the back as they departed. Now I was curious. Was this a good sign or bad? Maybe they were actually happy with my test scores? It could be!

As I sat for what seemed like an eternity but was probably just another fifteen minutes or so, the discussions in my head kept bouncing from one extreme to the other. *I failed. I passed. It's going to be OK. They'll give me another chance to take it. I passed, and I'll be on to the next step.*

Finally, the test administrator called the time and told everyone in the room to put their pencils down. Everyone handed their packets to the Marine at the front as they filed out into the hall. I was one of the first out the door, and I didn't have to go far. My recruiter was standing just outside the entrance waiting for me.

This meeting felt completely different from our encounter just a few hours before, when the recruiter had whisked me like a piece of livestock to the testing slaughterhouse. Now, Sergeant Q. held a box of juice in one hand and a cup of coffee in the other as he asked me to please follow him. We entered his office, and he motioned to a chair at the front of his desk. Placing both beverages before me, he asked, "Cream and sugar?"

"Yes, thank you," I replied as I settled in.

Sergeant Q. reached into his top desk drawer and pulled out a few packets of sugar and powdered creamer. As I poured the packets into my hot beverage, changing its color from dark brown to creamy white, he asked me what job I wanted in the Air Force.

"A nurse," I said.

He turned to his desk computer. "A wonderful choice," he said as he punched in a few keystrokes. "Your test scores actually are high enough to choose any position in the Air Force."

I smiled as I began to sip the coffee, then winced as the bitter liquid passed over my taste buds. My mind registered the flavor of the coffee by its rich earthy smell, but my mouth cried out in pain as the overheated, over brewed, extremely bitter sample burned my tongue. Sergeant Q. asked if everything was alright.

"My dad sells coffee," I replied. "He could set you up with a better product." I wasn't trying to insult him or his cup of joe. I really was trying to offer him a more pleasant future as I thought, *He drinks this stuff every day? Poor guy!* He never did follow up on my offer, but he also didn't seem to mind as I set the cup aside and looked eager to discuss my nursing options.

To be eligible for a nursing position, it turned out, you needed to have a college degree. So much for scoring high enough to take any job! Actually, my score was the highest they had seen on this relatively new version of the ASVAB. I surmised that was why I got the stare-down earlier in the testing room. Even though I could not apply for nursing, the recruiter understood my desire to be fully employable with a high-paying job at the end of my contract, so he looked through the available positions and strongly recommended that I go into aircraft power plant repair.

"Interesting. No, I don't think so," I immediately replied. But he continued, telling me that aircraft mechanics had unionized jobs, which were good ones to consider because of the two major airports in the Chicago area. As a woman, I would be a minority, he said, and would be easily employable at a very good rate of pay. I might have shown some interest as I shifted in my seat, so he pressed on.

My test scores showed a remarkable propensity toward mechanics, he told me, so I would pick it up easily. All training would be provided. The smoke was probably exiting my ears as my "mechanically adept" brain grinded like ungreased gears.

I had done no research on any jobs in the maintenance field. I had worked with a few basic hand tools while helping my dad around the house, but the tools I enjoyed using were microscopes, centrifuges, and scales.

The recruiter must have been good at his job, or I must have felt extremely vulnerable and concerned that it was a take it or leave it moment, because I agreed and signed a contract. I would do four years of active duty and two years of reserves, and receive free college tuition when I got out, should I desire to change careers at that time. I asked very few questions. I think I left in a daze, because I don't remember the 'L' ride home. But I was now enlisted in the United States Air Force!

That night at dinner, my parents had mixed reactions to my surprise announcement. My mother was happy to help out with my girls, her first grandchildren, during the day, but I hadn't thought through how she would feel about watching them full time for several months. I'd have to leave them with her as I attended basic training and advanced training for my new career as an airplane mechanic. Mom did not warmly receive the idea, but she was understanding of our plight and my desire to get ahead.

After I explained the highlights of the job, which included a union wage and my minority status as a woman in the military, she became much more accepting. Her father and brother were union men, and as a family, we knew about the strength in unions. Meanwhile, it surprised my stepdad that I had chosen the Air

Force and not the Army like he had. But my strange career field did not surprise him. "It's a brilliant choice, and you'll be great at it," he told me.

My girls, three-and-a-half-year-old Jean Marie and two-year-old Kymberly, were too young to know what was going on. I hoped it would be easier on them at this age, since they were all about playing games, and I still had brothers and sisters at home who loved taking them to the park and on walks or just liked hanging out with them in the yard by the cherry tree and kiddie pool.

Meanwhile, I thought long and hard about how to tell my soon-to-be ex. He was very tight with money, and in the months leading up to the court case, we had argued over the cost of food, clothing, school, and medical expenses for the children. I thought that if I brought an offer to the table that would require him to only pay the bare minimum in child support, he might be very willing to agree to everything in court.

4

LITA: RECRUITERS DON'T LIE

THE NEXT STEP WAS OUR court hearing. I arrived a bit early with the great news to share with my attorney to relay to the other side. He said it sounded like a good deal, which indicated to me that things were finally moving in the right direction.

About an hour later, we entered the courtroom and stood in front of the judge with the agreement ready to be signed. The floor dropped out when I saw my husband smirk and cross his arms over his chest.

"When will I see the girls if you are in San Antonio, Texas?" he asked.

We had just agreed that I would fly home with them over the summer so that they could alternate between my family and Pete's. I started to speak, but my lawyer hushed me and asked for a minute to finish up this loose end. The judge allowed us to step into the hall.

"What are you doing? Why are you being stubborn?" I cried.

Pete just smirked again and turned away as his attorney told mine that our deal was off. I could join the Air Force, but I would have to give up custody of the girls! My pulse quickened, my fists balled, and my voice rose to a near scream for the remainder of the conversation. I lit up like a firecracker! Oh yes, I can blow a gasket when pushed past my limits!

The two lawyers walked back into the courtroom, leaving Pete and me alone in the hall. Our lawyers returned with a new document, a continuance for thirty days. It was now September 1976, and I felt like my life was over. With the continuance in hand, I left.

I needed to decide what I wanted to do: negotiate with the unreasonable man I was trying to divorce or give up my hopes of starting out on a better footing after a career in the service. I went home for the day, not wanting to deal with the tension any longer.

The following day, I returned to the recruiting office. I explained what had happened: that I could not join with my girls, and that I refused to go anywhere without them!

Sergeant Q. said, "Well, since you have an outstanding court date, we can negate your contract and you can go on your way. Best of luck to you." Or maybe he said, "Sorry it turned out this way." I don't remember. I was in mental shock. All I could do was trudge down the hall, out the door, and onto the 'L' to return home.

My family was supportive, but there was nothing anyone could say that would make me feel less defeated. That month disappeared in a second, and I was once again inside City Hall's courtroom for marriage dissolution. Anger filled my heart and mind as I walked through the courtroom doors. My lawyer got up from the table at the front of the room, where he had been sitting with the other attorney. He took my elbow and led me back into the hall.

"Pete has changed his mind," my attorney said. "He said it is a good idea for you to join the United States Air Force as he will have less financial responsibility."

"Are you fucking kidding me?!" I practically shouted, using a word I didn't typically reach for. "Really?" I continued, "So now what?" My mind raced. The lawyer asked if I could go back to the Air Force and re-enlist. I didn't know, but I agreed to try.

As I left the courtroom, I could see Pete sitting in the back row on the left side. I glared at him but continued without a word.

Court was recessed until one p.m., so I had to hightail it to the recruiting office. The courthouse was in the center of the city, while the recruiting office staked its spot on the far southeastern part of the downtown area. It took two buses, but I arrived at the recruiting office in less than an hour.

I knocked on Sergeant Q.'s door and asked if I could speak with him. He motioned me in, and I took a seat. I started talking. He looked a bit bewildered after my explanation, but didn't show any emotion, so I wasn't sure what he would say.

Calmly, he said, "By law, now that the Air Force knows you are getting a divorce, we can't have you enlist. We don't accept single parents." Just then, another recruiter was walking past the office and Sergeant Q. jumped up and said, "Wait here." He hurried past me to reach the man in a dark green pair of pants with a white button-down shirt and medals and ribbons much like his own.

A few minutes later, he returned with the new man in tow. "Lita, this is Sergeant B. from the Army. He can help you out. Go sit and talk with him for a while, and I'll come by in a few minutes."

Sergeant B. politely shook my hand with a well-muscled forearm that told me he worked out a lot! We walked across the hall to the Army recruiting office, and he pulled out a seat for me in front of his desk. He explained that Sergeant Q. had informed him briefly about all that had happened and that they had agreed they would be willing to "bend the rules" a bit to help me get into the service, earn my college degree, and have a career and medical benefits for the girls.

With that, he asked me for my Social Security number. I dug it out of my wallet and handed it to him. No, I didn't know what it was at that point! For any prior-service readers, I'm sure you can recall a time in your life when you didn't know your SSN. He typed the number into his desktop computer, probably an IBM 5100. He looked through my recent ASVAB test results and looked up smiling.

"Lita! You should be a mechanic!"

Why do these recruiters keep saying that? I thought. *What on earth? Is there a drastic need for mechanics? Do they try to lead everyone in that direction to fulfill a quota?*

"Really?" I said.

He continued, "Your scores in the maintenance field are off the charts! And the Army is trying to integrate women into fields that were previously occupied only by men."

"What do you say?" a voice behind me asked. Sergeant Q. had just entered the room.

I half smiled and said, "You two have a bet going, don't you?" Sergeant B. explained the career choice he proposed, and Sergeant Q. gave him and me a "thumbs-up." I stared at his thumb and couldn't help but think of my dad, who always gave us a thumbs-up when he wanted to show his pride in each of us. At one point, my seven brothers and sisters and I had a bet going on about who could collect the most thumbs-ups from Dad in a month.

Suddenly, I found myself answering Sergeant Q.'s question. "Yes!" I almost yelled. "How do we do it?"

Within half an hour, I signed a new contract and headed back to City Hall. As I took the buses back through the city, I glanced out the window at all of these people going to and from work, to and from shopping, maybe to the lakefront or a museum. *Do any of them have this much trouble with their marriages? With their lives?* I wondered.

I arrived back at City Hall with half an hour to spare. I had NO intention of speaking with anyone until the judge asked, "Do you want to divorce this man?" So I hid out in the lobby for another fifteen minutes. Then I took the elevator up with many lawyers, and we all exited on the same floor.

My courtroom stood around the corner. I went in and asked my lawyer to come out to the hall to talk. Once there, I explained the new situation and he said it would take a couple of minutes to make changes to the documents to reflect that the "Air Force" was now the "Army," San Antonio, Texas, was now Fort Jackson, South Carolina, and the date of basic training was now January 17, 1977.

I went back into the courtroom, and the two attorneys went into a small room adjacent to the main courtroom with floor to ceiling glass walls dividing the two areas. They sat at a table, feverishly scribbling on the paperwork. When they finished, they beckoned both Pete and me. I was closest and entered, not bothering to hold the door for Pete, who was behind me.

Quick comments were made, heads nodded in agreement, we both signed the documents and walked back into the courtroom as the bailiff announced the arrival of the judge. Rather than taking our seats again, we simply walked up to the area immediately in front of the judge overseeing the case.

The lawyers spoke, the judge read, nodded a couple of times, and then directed his question to me. "Are you joining the Army to run away?"

"No, sir," I replied. "The Army will provide me with a career and an education so that I can better take care of my girls."

He nodded, looked at Pete, and asked if he agreed to this voluntarily. "Yes, Your Honor," he said. And with that, we were divorced.

You might think I would have been happy at this point. I might have been, but it doesn't register in my mind as one of the happiest times of my life. One of the most frustrating? Yes!

I traveled home on the 'L,' reading the documents I signed that day while the train made its way through the city. I was now divorced and a member of the U.S. Army! Damn! I call that a pretty good day! I forgot the many hour-long delays, and I hadn't yet told my mother or father about the trip back and forth to the recruiter, so they'd be in for a surprise.

My mom was at home watching my girls, and my dad was off selling a good tasting coffee, hopefully to the Army. I picked up some flowers at the small florist on Oak Park Avenue at my 'L' stop and walked the final seven blocks to my parents' home swiftly. My mom was happy to see the flowers.

"It's finally over?" she asked. "It took a long time. I was worried!" This was the 1970s, pre-cell phone and instant communication.

I quickly explained the changes and shocked my mother as I almost giddily sang, "I'm in the Army now!"

She was in the middle of cooking dinner, so she couldn't really talk much. She just asked if I could go down the street to get my sister and my girls, who were at the playground. Off I went, bringing the good news to three more family members. Over dinner, we discussed the day's events in detail. My dad was thrilled that I had chosen the Army. We then laid out the plan for the next year.

I wouldn't leave for basic training for another four months. That would be my save-up and train-up time. I had gotten two jobs at the local mall to afford living on my own, but my folks suggested I move back in with them and save money on rent. I would pitch in for food. This would allow me to save several thousand dollars for our first duty station move the following year.

I also had to get ready physically. I rode a bike often because I didn't own a car, but the recruiter said I had to pass a test that included running, sit-ups, and push-ups. I had never been a runner. My employment was fourteen miles away. I typically rode my bike there or took a bus. I decided to start running short stints and walk the rest of the way home every day.

Initially, the fourteen-mile trip on foot took longer than it did by bus, which interrupted meal time with my family. By the end of three months, however, I was running the required two miles plus another two miles, and I was power walking the rest. I was able to cut the trip down considerably by the time I quit, just before Christmas. I decided to quit a few weeks before I left in order to spend more time with my girls.

Another factor that strengthened me physically before shipping out involved the weather. 1976 was one of the worst winters in Chicago history, and I was out every day running or walking in it. The temperature did not rise above thirty-two degrees fahrenheit from December 28 through February 8. Lake Michigan was ninety percent frozen over the course of that winter, and so were my feet. I added push-ups and sit-ups to my routine slowly, so by the time I had to go, before the Chicago winter was over, I was ready!

5

LITA: BASIC TRAINING FOR PANSIES

TO BE TOTALLY HONEST, I do not remember how I got to Fort Jackson. I assume I flew down, but this part of the timeline is lost to me. When I did arrive, I was alone for the first short period of time. I know I was running across an open field when someone in uniform yelled at me to stop.

I complied and waited for this individual to walk up to me. When he came closer, he asked me what the hell I thought I was doing. I told him I was looking for a building where new people were supposed to meet up, and had gotten lost. I did not offer to shake his hand, nor did I introduce myself, but the next words out of his mouth made me sure I had made a huge mistake.

"YOU DO NOT run on my grass, is that understood?"

His grass? Who the heck was this guy, the landscaper? I wondered.

"OK," I replied. "I'm sorry I was on your grass."

"You were sorry, *SIR*! You will address me as sir!"

"OK, sir."

"Now drop and give me ten."

Ah! I knew this! My dad had told me about this! Finally! Something that made sense! I got down in the grass in what my dad had said was a pretty good push-up position, then I quickly did a push-up. But the man stopped me. "Sound off, soldier!" he yelled.

I looked up. "What does that mean, sir?"

"I want to hear you call out every push-up."

I completed the ten push-ups, sounding off as I did. Then I stood up with a smile for having accomplished them.

"Who told you to get up?" he barked. "No one."

"I was done with the ten push-ups. Isn't that what you wanted me to do?" I said, quickly slipping in a "sir."

"You will get up when you are told to recover!" the young man yelled. "Another ten, NOW!"

Oh crap! I thought. We were really getting somewhere, so I got back on my hands and knees, stretched out my legs, and did another ten push-ups as I sounded off with each one. Then I stopped and looked up to see if I could get up yet.

"Who are you looking at? Eyes front!"

I turned my head back so I was looking half at grass and half at a building. Once my head was back in line with my body, the man yelled, "Recover!" and I got back to my feet. I really did not know what to do next. He started walking away, and I was still on "his damn grass" that I had to run to get off of, but I chose to go across the street and run up it instead of taking a shortcut I knew.

As I approached the building, I spotted dozens of other new arrivals in rows along its side. New arrivals were so obvious to spot. Besides their civilian clothing, they looked as terrified as me. They weren't standing, however. They were lying on their backs and arms with their legs pushed toward the sky.

I ran right up to them and looked for whoever was "in charge." I apologized for being late, being sure to add the "sir" at the end.

"SIR?! Do I look like an officer? When you see this hat, you will refer to me as Drill Sergeant. I work for a living! Is that understood?"

"Yes, Drill Sergeant," was all I could say.

"Now drop and give me ten!"

Oh SHIT! What the heck?! What was this crazy world I had walked into? After my ten push-ups, I stayed in the push-up position, waiting for him to tell me to get up. From where I was, I could easily see the other tortured souls lying on the ground in front of me. I could also see other soldiers, like the one looming over me, with big wide hats like Smokey the Bear, circling us like sharks preparing for an attack, and yelling, constantly yelling.

Was my cohort's pain worse than mine? My arms were shaking. My shoulder blades were on fire! Finally, the large-built man yelled, "Recover!" and I gradually got to my feet.

"Not quick enough! Drop for ten!"

What?! Not quick enough? There are rules on getting up from torture? I got back down and could only do three push-ups. I was spent. I was shaking everywhere with a combination of pain and lack of strength. I remember my dad telling me, "If you can't do any more, the least you can do is stay in the push-up position," so I did, until my arms shook so badly I fell on my face.

The drill sergeant wasn't looking. I pushed back up, not slowly and evenly as I was taught, but in a painful, jerky motion that would embarrass anyone knowing what a correct push-up was supposed to look like. But I got up, held it, and fell again. I called out, "Four, Drill Sergeant" and pushed up again although my shoulders and arms ached more than I thought was possible. "Five, Drill Sergeant."

"Recover!" he barked.

I quickly jumped to my feet. The remainder of the new soldiers also got up from their backs. By now I noticed two segregated groups, women and men. The group of women was maybe a third or a quarter of the size of the men's group, over a hundred in all.

The drill sergeant asked me for my last name.

"McNamara, Drill Sergeant."

"Fall in," he said. "Find a place in the formation."

I ran to the back of the group of women now lining up in four rows facing the sidewalk and stood next to another frightened girl. She was taller than me by almost six inches. She was Black and thin with tight curls and possessed a small case with her personal belongings. I had a backpack that I used for camping as a Girl Scout leader for my personal belongings. I wanted to say "Hi," but this was not the time or place. I just stood there waiting for the next bit of instruction.

I glanced at my watch: 8:32. Still early enough, I hoped, for breakfast. The large well-biceped drill sergeant—a Black man, I now noticed—was standing in front of the group of female recruits. How I had missed the details of his race and stature confused me for a minute. *I should be more aware of my surroundings*, I thought. *I will work on that personal fault in the future.* But for now, I was trying to listen and make sense of what he was yelling.

"You will be getting your gear from that supply room at the top of the stairs."

Just as he said that, the doors opened. "File out from the right, starting with the row in front. I want this orderly. I want no talking in line. No talking unless you are asked a question, do you understand me?"

"Yes, Drill Sergeant," we all yelled, almost in unison.

"File out!"

We moved in an orderly fashion, starting with the first of the four rows. I was the last to enter the building. The first thing we saw was a warehouse setup with long counters. Soldiers stood about six to ten feet apart behind the counters . The first soldier handed us a duffle bag.

"Your gear goes inside. Take this sheet and initial as you get your gear," he said. He handed each of us a piece of paper with a list of supplies we were soon to be adding to our bag.

This made sense to me. We simply walked across the warehouse floor, stopping at each station where a different soldier stood handing us a different piece of gear, mess kit, sleeping bag, GP tiny with poles (a general purpose piece of green canvas that would make half of a tent), backpack, canteen, canteen cup, some waterproof clothing, socks, then uniforms. They simply looked at each of us and yelled what they thought our size would be over their shoulder: "Medium long. Small short. Large long."

Other soldiers closer to large bins in the rear of the warehouse would reach into the various piles and grab green pants and shirts out of mountains of clothing and toss them forward. At one station, they asked about our shoe size. "Seven and a half," I said. A soldier grabbed two pairs of black calf-high boots and plunked them onto the counter in front of me. My bag was almost full. Several more stations to go. I kept pushing the gear down to make more room for the equipment. When we were finally finished, my duffle bag was HEAVY!

We received two padlocks and were told to exit and re-form in the courtyard behind the building. The drill sergeants were there waiting, encouraging us to line up in their ever-so-pleasant manner. It was here that I took notice of the second drill sergeant, a younger, heavily tanned Caucasian man with a medium build. The quiet one. We lined up and stood still, awaiting further instructions, our duffle bags at one side, our personal gear from home on the other.

The instructions were always short, concise, and exact. Line up, file out, move out, rows of two, double time, drop for ten. I guess it kept things easier. You knew you had to listen as soon as the drill sergeant's mouth opened. We had two: Drill Sergeant Johnson and Drill Sergeant Dugger. Johnson, the medium-build one, was about thirty and looked to have never had a beard. I imagined a smooth baby face.

Drill Sergeant Dugger, on the other hand, was huge and towered over us. This burly Black man had a small moustache over a stern, hard-set scowl, black-rimmed glasses, and a large, ragged scar that ran down the side of his arm from his elbow to his wrist.

A blue and silver pin sprung from Sergeant Dugger's chest, and he carried a rifle with a wreath encircling it part way from the bottom. I didn't know what it was for, but it looked odd, as the blue and silver stood out starkly against his dark green uniform. I hadn't seen it before, and I wanted to find out what it was about. I made a mental note to research it in the future.

The sun was up now, and the heat was starting to reflect off the concrete on which we were standing. Steam rose off the grass behind the two drill sergeants. I was praying we wouldn't have to do more push-ups, as my arms were still aching, and I now had this overstuffed duffle bag to haul around.

Sergeant Dugger started speaking, giving massive amounts of instructions that I wondered how we would ever remember. He spoke about attention to detail, and specifically gave times we were to leave for meals, pick up linens, store gear, and go to classes or medical. I hoped he would remind us, because I had already forgotten what he'd said.

"Move out. File in two rows." He motioned for us to split up. Every other "new soldier" split off along the sides of the road until we were now in two lines, facing away from the sun on a narrow sidewalk that led to another warehouse. We all strained under the weight of our duffle bags, hoisted on our backs, and carried our personal gear in our left hands.

My helmet was hitting my lower back every time I took a step, which was more inconvenient than painful. But my upper arms really hurt. We arrived at the new warehouse building with the label "Linens" emblazoned on it and received an instruction to stop.

"HALT!" Sergeant Johnson commanded.

We stopped and wondered if we should put the bags down.

"File in from the right. Move!" Sergeant Dugger next commanded.

Well, that answers that question, I thought.

We entered the barn doors and saw another long counter with soldiers behind it. Again, a check sheet: two white towels, one washcloth, two white sheets, two green blankets. We initialed a receipt and quickly filed out of the other set of doors and back onto the concrete in front of Sergeant Dugger. Now we had sheets and blankets in one arm, hugged to our chests, and our left arms hung by the side with personal gear. Meanwhile, the duffle bags, still on our backs, caused more intense pain.

"Stay in single file. Move down to Sergeant Johnson at the end of the road."

"Yes, Drill Sergeant!" we shouted as we trudged down the narrow walkway.

"Double time!" Sergeant Dugger yelled, and we started moving at a quicker pace, mimicking a run. Maybe a slight uneven jog. We had difficulty stopping when we reached the end. The momentum of the weight we were carrying wanted to push us into the person in front of us.

I was lucky. Still, toward the end, I saw the commotion ahead of me and slowed down before I collided with the duffle bag I had been following. We stood for a minute catching our breath. I thought, *What time is it? We haven't had breakfast yet! I'm starving!*

"Fall in! I want four lines, starting at Sergeant Johnson over there, facing the building. Leave your packs on. Move!"

I wasn't paying attention. I was thinking about eating, but I heard the last part, "move," so I started following the person in front of me. We ended up in four rows of twelve girls. I could call us women, as I was twenty-three, after all, had already been married, and had two little girls at home. But looking at these scared faces around me, I knew that we were girls.

I stood in the last row, second from the end now. I was happy to have moved up a spot. It felt uneasy to be last. I worried I would always be called "the one who was last." *In the future, if given the chance,* I told myself, *I will move up to the front.* I wanted to excel, not hide in the back. I heard the drill sergeant again.

"This is your home for the next nine weeks. When I say fall out, I want you to bring your gear inside, put it in a locker, and lock that locker with one of your locks. Put your sheets and blankets on the foot of the bed and return to this formation. Is that understood?"

We all answered affirmatively, but trust me, I had questions! He yelled, "Fall out!" and we half ran, half tripped up the front steps and into the three-story brick building, a basic tan brick with rectangular windows lining each floor. I imagined that whoever built it had thought, *there will be soldiers living here in the same neat, orderly way that they train outside.*

We encountered double metal doors propped open to the entrance of the building. Painted stones at the base of each door held them open. I think they had sayings like "Victory Starts Here" on them. Three concrete steps led up to the doors, and I could see more concrete stairs inside leading to the upper floors. These were solid, clean, stern, unyielding stairs that I was sure would take a toll on feet, ankles, and knees as time went on.

Sergeant Dugger stood just inside the doorway with his arms folded over his chest. "First floor and first floor *only.* Eight to a room. File into the first room first and if it's full, move to the next one till you have a bunk. Do not lie on the bunk. Do not put anything on your bunk but your sheets. Gear in the lockers, lock on the locker, then fall back here. Make it quick. MOVE!"

We fell into the first-floor hallway, where we saw six overly large rooms, with eight single steel-frame beds in each. There was a tall locker next to each bed. The black and white striped mattresses looked like they needed to be incinerated, and the pillows looked as tired as I felt. I assumed the first rooms would be full, but with a glance, I spotted an empty bed in one of them, near a window no less, and walked right in. I placed my sheets and blankets at the foot of the bed, and turned to the locker.

After shoving my gear into a bulging locker, I secured it with the padlock, put the key in my pocket, and ran out of the room into the formation of a dozen or so girls. Now I stood in the second row, feeling much better already.

Once everyone was out on the pavement, Sergeant Johnson looked at his watch and then at us. He said, "We do NOT have all day, and I expect you to move with a purpose when I say move," or something like that.

The bottom line was, we were now late for lunch. *Lunch?! Yes!*

Sergeant Johnson yelled attention, at which point most of us stood straighter in our lines. He then called over a female soldier who was working on weeding in front of the building.

As she started running over from her landscaping details, she looked very angry, but when she got in front of the drill sergeant, she wore no expression at all. She yelled, "Private Paulson reporting, Drill Sergeant," and she stood very erect in front of him and in front of all of us.

"I am going to show you once how I want you to move," Sergeant Johnson said. "When I say 'attention,' I want your heads up, eyes front, shoulders back and squared, arms hanging loosely along your side, hands curled into a loose fist, thumb on the outside, not across the fingers, not inside of the fingers, on the outside edge like this." He held his hand up. "Legs bent slightly at the knees. Do not lock your knees, feet at a forty-five-degree angle. This soldier will demonstrate. Attention!"

The girl he had picked popped up sharply and looked very soldierly.

"Right face," he yelled, and the girl shifted one foot, turned to the right, and slid her other foot over to meet the first one with a bit of a snap. *Damn good!* I thought.

"OK. Back to your detail. Fall out!" and with that, the girl ran back to the safety of the weeds. Sergeant Johnson faced us once more. "Attention! Right face," he yelled, and we all did some version of what the sergeant wanted. Meanwhile, Sergeant Dugger walked between the rows, making corrections as he did. Once we were all in lines that he found acceptable, he yelled, "Forward, march."

Some of us started walking with our left foot first, some with our right. We looked sloppy, and he was angry. Once we got to the dining hall, he stopped us by yelling again. Given how much they yelled, I wondered if they ever lost their voices. We filed in one row at a time to a cafeteria where we each took a tray and were handed a plate with food on it. We were told to take two cartons of milk, and we found seats at the side where we had entered.

I ate quickly. I saw people in uniforms eating quickly, taking their tray and putting it on a moving belt along one wall that swiftly moved the trays out of sight. Lunch was over, and it was on to the next step. The day dragged on like this with a great amount of uncertainty hanging over everyone's heads.

Is this all there is? I thought. *Are we just in a prison of some type?* There was no talking, only yelling. There was no real education taking place, unless you counted what we learned by first doing something wrong, dropping for ten, and trying like hell not to do wrong again!

Day one ended with the forty-eight of us showering together under a handful of jet sprays from posts scattered in a room off of the toilet area. We were required to sleep in T-shirts and our olive drab (OD) green pants. The T-shirts had also been handed out as part of our supply ration. All other gear was stored in the lockers already. We had hung our uniforms, learned how to polish our boots, and realized our personal clothes no longer had meaning here. I slept soundly.

At four thirty in the morning, a metal can clanging against the wall woke us up to a shock. We were to form up outside in two minutes. Everyone grabbed a shirt and ran down the hall as they were still closing the flies of their pants they had slept in last night. I was one of the first ones out, and I was now in the front row. I stood shaking from the cold, still half asleep.

"Too SLOW!" I heard. This must have been a drill sergeant, but I didn't recognize the voice. "Drop and give me twenty!"

Well that's a crappy way to wake up, I thought. I started the push-ups, sounding off with each one. At first I didn't notice, but toward the end it dawned on me that I was the only one still going. I hesitated and then stopped at eighteen. I could have completed the rest, but a gut instinct told me that forty-seven enemies would appear if I did. Rather than finish the assignment, I started shaking like the other girls who were in various stages of trying to stay up off the ground.

"Recover," the man barked. "Get back inside, and get the rest of your clothes on! I want you back out here in five minutes!"

We all ran back in. A couple of my platoon mates shot me ugly stares, and I really started to worry about whether I would be seen as a kiss-ass. I watched the others as I finished dressing. I now had the time to put on a pair of knee-length OD green wool socks, boots I had polished the previous night, a belt, a field jacket, and black leather gloves with OD green wool liners.

I tried to time it so that I was never the first one out again and never did more push-ups than the group. Sergeant Dugger noticed this ploy and gave me extra push-ups whenever he felt bored, I think, or perhaps this was in my head. Mind games abounded here.

Despite it all, I was determined to succeed, but I already missed my daughters terribly. By the end of week one, I was almost in tears in the evening as I lay in bed staring at the ceiling. The following day, we were allowed to go to chapel service as a group, and I poured my heart out at the simple cross at the front of the warehouse. I prayed for strength. There was no Mass, no official service of any denomination, just a man with a silver cross on his collar leading us in prayer.

It turned out to be a very easy day. Our only task was to spit shine our boots. I don't remember who gave us instructions. I rubbed the black wax into the leather. Mine didn't have the best shine, but I was sure that they would pass inspection. We also were shown how to set up our lockers, roll our clothes, even the underwear, and store them so every locker looked alike.

I appreciated the break, and noticed that the drill sergeants' office door was open. I hesitated but then bravely walked the few steps from my room to the office and knocked on the door. Sergeant Dugger looked up from the paperwork on his desk.

"What is it, McNamara?"

I asked if I could mail something home to my children. We had had the opportunity to call home that day, but my girls were with their father for the first court-ordered visitation. Sergeant Dugger said the mailbox was at the door. I told him I knew that, but they were young and a letter might not be very exciting for them. I told him that I wanted to get them something at the store.

We were allowed to go to the post exchange (PX) to pick up stationery, personal hygiene supplies, shoe polish, and the like. I had seen that they had modeling clay, and I wondered if I could go back to get it for my girls.

"No, that is contraband," Sergeant Dugger said.

We were not allowed to purchase anything except the items on our approved list. I felt brokenhearted, but left with a simple, "Yes, Drill Sergeant" and returned to my boots.

The second week flew by, and I was relieved when I got to talk to my girls. After the call, however, I experienced some kind of emotional breakdown. I could not stop crying. It was a painful, deep cry of pure anguish. All I could think was that I was not going to see my girls again.

Soon, I was called into the drill sergeants' office. I reported as instructed.

I was almost unable to hold my head erect. Tears flowed down my face, and my nose ran like crazy. Someone had reported that I had been sobbing. Sergeant Dugger stood behind the desk between us and handed me a box of tissues.

Sergeant Johnson had been sitting in a corner and looked up with surprise. "What's the problem, McNamara?"

I told him I missed my girls and wanted to go home. He looked at Sergeant Dugger and back at me. "Do you want to make a call to the chaplain?" Sergeant Johnson asked.

"I don't know," was all I could say.

With that, Dugger motioned his head toward Johnson, who stood and said, "Come with me, McNamara."

I followed him out of the office, and we walked quickly down the walkway to the building we had prayed at earlier. He told me to wait outside, and I took a position of parade rest as he walked in. This is a way to stand tall: your hands crossed at the small of your back with your eyes forward as you don't speak or move. I called it "statue," because I really felt like I was pretending to be a statue. But I was doing a pretty lousy statue right then with the tears streaming down my face and my eyes welling up with an endless supply to replenish those I had lost to the pavement between my boots.

After I had stood like that for a few minutes, Sergeant Johnson opened the door and called me in. The chaplain was a young man, maybe thirty-five years old. I had no idea what denomination he belonged to, as our prayers at the last service had all been very generic. He smiled and asked me to come in and sit down. I did, and Sergeant Johnson said he would be back in twenty minutes.

The chaplain immediately said he had been told I was having problems with my adjustment, and he might be able to help. In between sobbing like a baby, I explained the whole situation. As

I did, he handed me a box of tissues. I thanked him and tried to control myself.

Some of what I told him surprised him. Not many recruits had family problems already. How was it that I was divorced, with children, in the Army? I remembered the sleight of hand the recruiters had pulled to get me in.

"I was divorced *after* I joined," I told the chaplain. "I was in the delayed enlistment program and had already signed the contract before I got divorced." Technically, this was true, even if it was only by a few hours.

The chaplain said that the first few weeks were usually the hardest for all recruits. His door was always open. If I needed to drop by, he said, all I had to do was ask to see him or any other chaplain on duty. He reassured me that my feelings would ease up in just a few days. I thanked him and stood to leave as I saw Sergeant Johnson walking toward the office.

The two soldiers nodded at each other, and the drill sergeant smiled slightly as the chaplain told him he was doing a great job. *Probably the only smile I'll ever see on his face*, I thought as we double-timed back to the barracks. My platoon was in the front leaning rest or push-up position out in front of the building. I immediately "fell in" to my assigned spot in the first squad (the first row of soldiers in my platoon). I jumped down to the ground and just started knocking them out, quickly catching up to the group's twenty-fifth exercise.

"Twenty-six, Drill Sergeant. Twenty-seven, Drill Sergeant. Twenty-eight, Drill Sergeant. Twenty-nine, Drill Sergeant. Thirty, DRILL SERGEANT!" we all yelled in unison.

"Recover," Sergeant Dugger said, and we all jumped to our feet yelling, "We like it. We love it. We want more of it! GRRRRRRRR!" We had picked this up from the men's platoon activities we could easily observe adjacent to ours. They lived on the second and third floors of our barracks. We were not allowed to talk to them or look at them, and the general impression I got was that we probably shouldn't even think about them! I would later learn we were the first integrated training company for Basic Combat Training at Fort Jackson, and Drill Sergeants Johnson and Dugger had felt slighted by drawing the short straw and having to train us instead of the men.

The next two weeks actually whizzed by, and I was more at ease with being away from home. What you say to a priest is supposed to be confidential, but I sensed that the chaplain had talked to my drill sergeants, because they began treating me just a bit differently.

They knew I could compete physically with the younger girls and that I might even outdo some of them. And my age made me a kind of den mother to many of the girls in my platoon and all the girls in my squad. I always lent an ear if they were feeling low, and I helped with boot polishing techniques and sheet stretching on the bunks. I also helped them with any classroom instruction as we lay in our bunks after hours. I was happy to go over the information again, since I always took notes.

Around this time, a girl in our platoon died by suicide. She was from the third squad, quiet and withdrawn, and had hung herself in the shower room. I didn't know her personally, but we all took her death very hard. The next morning, the chaplain came to our barracks and spoke to us semi-formally as a group.

We sat on the pavement in a circle around the young man as he stood and shared comforting words. He said it pained him that the recruit did not feel she could go to him or someone else for help. Real pain emanated from his eyes. He meant every word, though he did appear somewhat focused on how her death impacted him personally.

"Please, " he implored. "If any of you know of anyone in this kind of mental stress that makes them feel they just can't go on, please come and get me."

We simply nodded. That was all anyone ever said to us about her death.

The weekend after this traumatic event, Sergeant Dugger asked who had detail the following Monday. Detail was extra duty that you performed on top of the actual scheduled activities and classes.

I was on, so I yelled, "I do, Drill Sergeant," and he told me to fall out of formation.

I came to attention, took a step back, performed a facing movement, and marched out of my formation as the others in my platoon covered down, or took my place. I reported to the drill sergeant, and he told me to go to the office. There, I saw two men from the other platoons waiting. We all stood at parade rest outside of the office.

When we were called in, we were told that our detail Monday was very special and we would need our dress greens—the uniform I didn't think I would wear until graduation. We were told to ask our platoon sergeants for instruction on setting up the uniforms.

"They will be pressed, and shoes will be polished. You will look sharp," said a drill sergeant I didn't recognize. "You will need your weapons, and they will be cleaned and inspected on Sunday. Is that understood?"

"Yes, Drill Sergeant," we said.

But *hell no* is what I was thinking.

On Sunday, Sergeant Dugger asked me if I had nylon stockings to wear with my class A's. No, I didn't. "You will go to the PX and purchase them after chow," he said, referring to the base exchange. And he dismissed me.

I went back to meet with the platoon sergeant who retrieved supplies, drove back and forth in a jeep, and seemed to have a lot of clerical duties. We had never interacted with him before. He instructed me on setting up my uniform, polishing the small brass pins that I affixed to the collars of my jacket and shirt, and placing my name tag. Afterward, he drove me to the BX, and I purchased the nylons.

As I stood in line, I saw the modeling clay near the checkout counter. I mentally struggled with right and wrong but purchased the clay anyway. When we got back to the barracks, I quickly wrapped the clay in the brown paper bag from the store and used extra stamps to hold it together. I put my girls' names on the front, my parents' address, and walked to the mail slot near the drill sergeants' office. It was a close fit, but I was lucky and the package slid into the slot.

After I put it in, I turned to return to my room when my eye caught Sergeant Dugger's. He was looking straight at me. I turned bright red but continued the few steps to my room. Back in my bunk, I tugged nervously at my sheets and blanket, making sure they were tight, and straightened my locker just a bit more. Guilt was just as good as push-ups, I imagined.

Monday morning was different, but only for me. I had to dress and report for chow at the same time as my platoon, but I was told to move to the front of the line with the two men also in dress uniform. Sergeant Dugger also wore a dress uniform, but it seemed to fit him more naturally than ours. Maybe the chest full of ribbons and medals made his look better.

We ate quickly, retrieved our weapons from the supply room, and waited outside for further instruction. Our weapons had already been inspected the day before, but just to make sure, Dugger inspected each one again. He told us to follow him, and we walked in file toward the vehicle parked behind the supply building.

We boarded the bus and noticed there were others like us already on board. These recruits did not have weapons, however. As we drove away, Sergeant Dugger said, "Give me your attention." We looked up, not knowing what to expect.

"You will be participating in a part of drill and ceremony that is a very important act you will do in this uniform," Sergeant

Dugger said. "You are going to be the Honor Guard for a soldier that was killed on duty. If you have a weapon, you will be firing volleys of blank rounds, and if you do not have a weapon, you will be carrying our soldier to the gravesite and folding his flag. We will be arriving on site two hours before the ceremony, which will give you time to learn your positions. Sergeant L. will instruct the rifle team. I will instruct the rest. We have a good two-hour drive. You can get some rest, but do not wrinkle your uniforms."

I turned to look out the window. This was a lot to take in. We were doing actual work today. We were going to represent the Army as this soldier was being laid to rest. I was feeling proud of this uniform. I hadn't felt the same in my OD green work uniform, but today, in this setting, I felt a definite sense of pride.

The trip home from the cemetery was quiet. All of the men slept soundly. Sleep was a luxury, and I probably should have taken advantage of the opportunity, but I didn't. I sat at the front of the bus, across the aisle from Sergeant Dugger. The men were all in the back, their jackets over the seat backs, their snores audible throughout the coach. I took a risk.

"Drill Sergeant Dugger," I started.

"Yes, McNamara." We were always addressed by our last names.

"What is the medal with the rifle on your uniform?"

He looked at me and smiled. Out of all the questions in the world, that one surprised him. It turned out to be a Combat Infantryman Badge. The badge is given to a soldier who was engaged in ground combat while assigned as a member of special forces, as a ranger, or in an infantry unit (a brigade size unit or smaller). I told him I respected the service that he had given and asked how he felt about being a drill sergeant.

"You're an odd duck, Mac," he responded.

I now had a nickname! I was Mac! It sounded "soldierly." The conversation continued for most of the trip home. The entire time

I talked about myself—where I'd been, what I'd experienced, and where I guessed I was going. During the discussion, I discovered that Sergeant Dugger was under some stress of his own. Ours was the first co-ed platoon to be trained, and the drill sergeants from the other platoons had been making fun of the assignment he had been given. I learned that to them, we were pansies, or weak and useless.

This knowledge gave me a new outlook on the training we were receiving. Perhaps we were being pushed harder to show that we were up to the task. As I contemplated the drill sergeants' position, I softened a bit. I thought of them as humans, as men, and as I did, I found other emotions surfacing that I had repressed for weeks since coming to Fort Jackson. I suddenly looked at Sergeant Dugger with admiration and desire! My feelings must have shown in my eyes as I stared at him across the bus aisle.

As I stared, he tilted his head slightly, curled his lip into a slight smile under his thick moustache, and winked! I must have looked like a holiday decoration with the bright red blush my face took on within the confines of my green Army uniform.

Unloading from the bus took place after lights were out for the rest of the platoon. The ceremony, luncheon with the family of the deceased soldier, and long drive back had taken longer than I expected. Sergeant Dugger released all of the other soldiers to their platoon representatives while he and I were left alone to lock the rifles in the supply room.

After ensuring they were locked securely, he asked, "Mac, you want a pop or something?" He reached into a small refrigerator and grabbed a beer, popping the cap and taking a long, cool swig.

"Would I be able to have a beer as well?" was my gutsy response.

"Hell yeah! Mac, you are a soldier's soldier. Don't let anyone hold you back! I mean it! I think you are going to do some pretty great things!" And he tossed me a beer. "We do NOT discuss this with your platoon! You were right to watch for them to be jealous of extra consideration. That's why I run you so hard."

We toasted the cans "to the Army and our fallen comrade," drank quickly to remove the day's heat, and then he reached over and kissed me on the lips. There was fire, passion, power, and strength in the kiss. He then sat back, drank the rest of his beer, and asked if I was in a hurry to hit the sack. I didn't have to think very hard about the answer, as I could easily see how hard the issue had gotten for him, straining on the dress green pants that already showed the well-defined muscles of his thighs.

We carefully yet quickly undressed and fell into each other's arms on a blanket he had hastily tossed on the floor. There were no words shared, only energy, pressing flesh against flesh, and straining muscles that were all too familiar to this front leaning rest position.

"Damn, Mac!" he finally said with an actual smile. I returned the smile, but still not knowing what to say, how to respond, what to call him. I didn't even know his first name! He must have known what was going on in my mind.

"John," he said, as he took my hand and kissed the back. "I am John Dugger. You can call me John if we are not in the company of others. We have to keep our decorum for the sake of training, but you already knew that."

6
LITA: SOME MORE ACTION

DAY ONE OF LIVE FIRE training on the rifle range had us all in a heightened state of excitement. We had been hauling around these weapons since our second week here, always having to clean them, guard them, perform drill and ceremony with them, but never fire them. But this was it!

The range was very muddy. We were coated in mud from the night's rain as we lay in a prone position trying to sight in a target 300 meters away. I successfully passed the course and quickly moved over to rest under a tree while waiting for the rest of the platoon.

The next event was a movement to contact, an offensive maneuver where two soldiers take turns firing at an objective (in this case, a dummy placed in a foxhole) while the other moves forward toward the target until they are close enough to engage it with a grenade (in this case, a dummy grenade). The rifle fire, however, consisted of live rounds, and we were judged by our accuracy as the instructors observed the dust jumping off the hill as we fired on the target objective.

They also judged us by how well we stayed concealed from possible enemy fire as we hopscotched forward. The final movement of one soldier running up into the target area to lob a grenade into the foxhole signaled to the other soldier to avert firing from the foxhole itself to another target off to the far left. Being the first one to the target, I ran forward to the base of the foxhole and lobbed the dummy grenade. As I did, however, I could clearly see dust kicking up around me, and I yelled at the top of my lungs, "Stop shooting at me!!"

Just as I began screaming, I also heard whistles blaring and observed Sergeant Dugger pouncing on the tip of my partner's rifle, pushing it into the mud. When he got up, mud covered him and his face flared red with rage. I don't remember what he said to the soldier, but trust me, his words were harsher than anything we had heard thus far. She was quickly taken aside, and two training soldiers from the range took over talking to her as Sergeant Dugger walked up to my position, still lying on the foxhole, shaking from head to toe.

"You all right, Mac?" he asked.

"Yes, Drill Sergeant," I said, and I jumped to my feet but quickly buckled again to my knees as they felt like rubber.

"Have a drink of water," he commanded, and I fidgeted with my canteen hanging on the side of my web belt. It took a few minutes, but I finally regained my sense of balance and stood upright.

"We don't have to do that again?" I asked, happily. For me, the answer was no. My partner in the exercise, however, was sent for remedial training. I never saw her again. By this point our platoon had diminished from the initial forty-eight to thirty-two. Various problems, mostly emotional or medical, caused the girls to drop out one by one. Undoubtedly, the omnipresent sexism also played a role.

One of the girls remaining had a last name with "Bunk" in it, so I called her Bunky. I was still Mac. A tall, wiry Black girl barely out of high school, she was also from the Chicago area. We became buddies, and shared stories at night before we sacked out.

One thing that girl could do was run. I had never seen a faster runner. She said it was a safety thing. "You gotta dodge them bullets," she explained, joking about the shootings in her neighborhood. These stories shocked me.

I had spent eight years in the Austin neighborhood, on the city's near west side. Since then, it has evolved into a high-crime area with low income, drugs, and yes, shootings. My family had relocated to the suburbs when I started high school. I hadn't realized it, being rather naïve at the time, but my parents likely moved when they believed the safety of our Chicago home was at risk.

At any rate, running to avoid being shot wasn't my goal. I just needed to pass the physical training (PT) test at the end of the cycle. We had to complete a two-mile run along with push-ups and sit-ups. The latter we did all the time as corporal punishment in formation. We almost never ran, however, and this worried me.

We were nearing the end of the training cycle. An overnight bivouac was scheduled along with a field march with full ruck (backpack with sleeping bag, a change of uniform, mess kit, tent half, and chemical suit), our rifle slung over a shoulder, and our web belt with canteen, flashlight, waterproof gear, decon kit, and medical kit. We were carrying thirty-five pounds and were ready to march twelve miles in the blistering South Carolina sun.

It was the end of February 1978, a few days after my birthday, and the daytime temperatures ranged in the seventies. But the sun and the movement with a full pack made it feel so much hotter. We were lined up along the sides of a dusty dirt road heading to the field. Separated by several meters between soldiers, we ended up in a very long line since we also had the two platoons of men with us.

The drill sergeants were scattered along the length of the company, in the center of the road. Us pansies were situated at the rear of the company. Sergeant Dugger's voice boomed as he called, "Mac!"

I ran forward, gear bouncing against my hips. "Yes, Drill Sergeant."

"You are our RTO (radiotelephone operator). Here is the PRC-10. (portable radio communication) You stay with me at the center," he said, and he hoisted the twenty-two pound radio on top of my rucksack.

Whoa! This was not going to be fun! I thought. "Yes, Drill Sergeant," I said.

"Move out!"

The orders started at the front of the company somewhere more than a block or so up the road and were relayed verbally back to the end of the element. Sergeant Dugger reached over my shoulder and turned a few dials. I heard a squeak, then he pressed the button and spoke into the handheld microphone attached via a coiled wire umbilical to the radio on my back. He then clipped the mike back to the side of my new baggage and motioned for our platoon to move out.

We stood in the center for a while, and Sergeant Dugger watched as the lines of my platoon mates, looking more than ever like stereotypical new female soldiers, walked past us hugging the tree line at the sides of the road as they were trained to do.

So what were we? Sitting ducks? This didn't seem like the smart thing to do. I guess in the training portion of the activity, this was appropriate as an instructor. I was sure if it were real-life combat, we would also be taking cover as we maneuvered forward.

Once half of our platoon had passed us, Sergeant Dugger started walking along with the company, but at a much slower pace. I was happy about this change, since the added weight was making it rather challenging even to walk upright. Occasionally, Sergeant Dugger would take the mike, say something to the drill sergeant on the other end, and then replace the mike. Once the last person in our platoon had passed us, he said, "OK, let's go," and started a slow jog down the middle of the road.

What the hell?! Was he kidding me? I started moving my legs in a way that should have been a jog but turned out to be a stiff-legged power walk. I had difficulty keeping my balance on the uneven ground. The added weight made it hard to keep up, but I kept trying, and I succeeded. When we had finally gotten to the front of our platoon, he stopped again, waiting for half of the troops to pass, then started walking slowly till we were at the end.

Again he said, "Let's go, Mac," and it repeated.

By the time we ended the forced road march at our bivouac site, I was exhausted. We had marched three hours, though we had taken a break midway to check for blisters, at which point I was able to stretch my shoulders and back.

The bivouac site was separated by terrain: men on one side of the road and ahead of some type of obstacle course set up, the women on the near side of the road where we had stopped. We were assigned bunkmates, and we learned how to set up our GP (general purpose) tinys. We were each issued a shelter half (piece of canvas with snaps), a tent pole, and stakes. The idea was to snap the two together and make a very low-to-the-ground tent you barely had room to crawl into.

Bunky and I set ours up under some cover of a tree with low-hanging branches. We put waterproof ground cloths down and unrolled our sleeping bags. It was getting dark, and my stomach reminded me it was time to eat. We took out our C rations, opened the can of "food," ate it without using our perfectly clean inspection-ready mess kits, drank some water, and stretched out for a few minutes.

Sergeant Johnson came by with some short pieces of rope, handed each of us a handful, and said, "Pass these out to the platoon. Everyone ties their weapon to their wrist before sleeping. If we come by and are able to take your weapon, you are going home with an Article 15 or a court-martial."

We took the lengths of rope and headed off in opposite directions. It was now very dark, and I had to watch where I was going to avoid poking my eye out on branches. I was just about done with my project when I accidentally stepped right into a foxhole that had been dug by troops sometime in the past.

The fall knocked me out. I had my steel pot of a helmet on my head, and I guess I hit my head on the way down as well as twisted my knee. The next thing I was aware of was Sergeant Dugger pulling me out of the foxhole by my load bearing equipment (LBE) and web belt. Coming to as he did so, I winced in pain. He and a couple of the members of my platoon were standing on the outside perimeter of the foxhole staring at me as if I were an alien.

A lump appeared above my eye and some blood trickled down my face. Sergeant Johnson had a flashlight trained on my head, then shifted the light up and down my body to check for other obvious injuries. Finding none, he said, "OK, Mac, you're just banged up."

He asked who else needed rope, jumped down into the hole to retrieve the remaining ropes, handed them out, and instructed everyone to go back to their tents. He would do roll call in a few minutes. Everyone needed to be in their tents.

I tried to stand and couldn't. My knee was very sore, and I sat back on the ground immediately. I told Sergeant Dugger I thought I needed a medic. He felt the knee through the pant leg and even I could see the swelling was pushing against the fabric, making the once loose pant leg unable to shift away from my leg.

"Shit," he said, then used the PRC-10 that he now had on his back to call a medic from the garrison.

The medics eventually came and hauled me to the hospital on the Fort. Bunky went with me. At the hospital, they examined my knee, gave me an ice pack and an aspirin, and told the medics to bring us back to the field. Once I was back, Sergeant Dugger took my sick slip and advised us to get some sleep because "tomorrow's going to be a hell of a day."

That night, I slept soundly even with the pain and the discomfort of sleeping completely dressed with full gear, web belt, LBE, and my rifle tied to my wrist. Sleeping in the woods felt peaceful. I had gone on many campouts as a Girl Scout, and had looked forward to them every year.

Early the next morning, we woke to a bright, sunny day with steam coming off the still-cool forest floor. Bunky asked how my knee was. I shrugged and said I would live, so we got our boots on, rolled up our gear, broke down the tents, and got ready for whatever was next, the "hell of a day" that our drill sergeant had promised us.

The sound of trucks barreling down the road was most welcome. "Load up!" called one of the drill sergeants, and we all moved toward the road to get into the back of the deuce and a half trucks—large multi-use trucks that can haul gear or personnel—with canvas backs and bench seats along each side of the bed. It hurt a little getting up onto the truck because the swelling in my knee didn't allow me to bend my leg fully. Once inside, however, I knew we were heading back to the garrison, the warmth of our barracks, a hot shower, and decent chow.

As the truck rumbled down the dirt road, I overheard a portable radio that the driver had in the cab of the truck. The news report stated that the Fort schools, bank, and exchange would be closed today due to excessive snow. Snow?

Bunky and I looked out through the gap in the canvas where it was tied to a metal frame that created a canopy for us. I looked at a distant hill and saw a slight coating of white that had stuck to the grass. Excessive snow?! I now laughed almost uncontrollably. It was the only time I laughed during basic training. I guess Sergeant Dugger wasn't used to snow. This wasn't a hell of a day. The storms that had fallen on my hometown of Chicago the past few weeks, now those were storms! With 8.8, 12.4, and 10.3

inches between January 12 and February 7, Chicago had suffered greatly that winter. It could have been worse. I would have had to shovel all of that snow if I had been home!

There was a lull for about one week, enough time to let my knee heal. We concentrated on coursework and passing different tests to measure what we had learned during our stay at Fort Jackson. The final week and a half was nonstop activity, however. It began with a five-mile run. We were back in the field on the same dirt road we had performed our field march on a week ago. Rather than having full ruck this time, we did not have equipment. Our weapons stayed locked up in the supply room, our gear back in our lockers. It was just our web belts, LBE, canteens, and the realization that basic training was almost over.

The two platoons of men were grouped on the road ahead of us. We were at the tail end, as usual, and we were told the trail would be marked. There would be some cross-country work, taking us through a safe (no foxholes) part of the forest. It was a timed run: five miles, on your mark, get set, whistle blown, and everyone started running.

Bunky and I had been running together whenever we had the opportunity to do so. She had helped me get my breathing under control, and my times improved dramatically. Somewhere halfway into the run, the two of us started passing members of one of the other platoons. By the time we were close to the end, without realizing it, we had already passed all of the second platoon and part of the first platoon.

We could see the finish line where the drill sergeants stood with stop watches and clipboards. We gave each other an agreeable nod and put every ounce of strength we had in us to race to the finish, passing one after another of the first platoon soldiers struggling to stay upright. As Sergeant Dugger saw us coming down the road running full tilt, he smiled so broadly his teeth could have given away our position to the enemy in a dense wood.

We both crossed simultaneously, with only a handful of the first platoon troops resting now after having come in before us. Bunky and I grabbed a tree and collapsed to catch our breath, then got back up and went to the finish line, waiting for the rest of our platoon to come in, cheering them on.

Following this all-out race to the finish, we had assumed we would be having a day of rest, or drill and ceremony with graduation just about a week away. We were physically spent, but content.

"Job well done," our drill sergeants told us.

But to our astonishment, the run was the beginning of a day chock-full of adventure after adventure. Our next task: Dig a regulation foxhole, a six-and-a-half-foot by three-foot rectangle, deep enough to be armpit high when you stood in it. We did not have to dig a grenade sump nor put a sandbag, log, or other protection at the front, nor did we have to put cover and concealment. As long as we could explain what we would do after we dug the pit, we would pass.

Following that was a low crawl under razor wire with tracers fired overhead. I couldn't tell how far overhead they were, but the sound of rounds coming my way motivated me to move quickly to the end. Lastly, there was a sandbag carry. I believe the bags weighed seventy-five pounds. We had to carry them twenty-five yards, drop them, run back, and get another, etc., until all four were moved from one side of the range to the other. After we accomplished all these tasks, we could eat lunch and rest before marching back to the barracks. I called this the day from hell.

Graduation was bittersweet. I was glad to be finished. I felt I had learned a lot and grown into a more capable person. But here again the recruiter played a hard trick on me. No, I didn't get "time off to go home before my next training assignment." We were driven to the train station and handed a ticket to our next duty station for training. In my case, this would be Aberdeen Proving Ground (APG) near Baltimore, Maryland.

Remember, the year was 1978. I had no cell phone, no way to mentally maneuver the world I was living in other than simply following orders. As I sat in the dining coach of the train with another recent graduate heading to Aberdeen, I once again started welling up with tears. I had looked forward to going home to be with my daughters for a break. Last time I had spoken to them on the phone, I had told them I would be home soon. Now I had orders for sixteen weeks of training in Maryland, and the grief and homesickness I felt were overwhelming.

My fellow soldier glanced at her orders, then at mine. "You know," she started, "it says here that we are to report for duty at 0700 Monday the twentieth. Today is Friday the seventeenth. Oh? Happy Saint Patrick's Day!"

I looked at her and took my orders back. Really? Could that be true? I read it, then reread it. I stopped crying and asked for a huge favor. Would she be willing to take my gear and store it till Sunday? I would come back on Sunday night. Did she want anything from Chicago? Thank you, thank you! "Washington D.C.," the conductor was calling out. "Washington, next stop." I jumped up, grabbed my hat, and walked to the train exit, stuffing my orders in my shirt pocket as I did.

The trip home was uneventful. Back then you could actually walk up to a ticket counter at the airport, tell them where you wanted to go, pay your money, and receive a ticket with a gate number. I boarded a flight as soon as I stepped into Washington Dulles airport, and we were wheels up in minutes. I was probably home before my duffle bag got to Aberdeen. From the airport I took a taxi home and walked into the house to see the banner that my girls had made: "Welcome Home, Mom," it said.

How did they know? Oh! I forgot. I hadn't even had a chance to tell them that the Army had changed my plans, and that I almost didn't come home at all! But here I was, and there they were, and the tears and hugs lasted well into the night.

7

LITA: ADVANCED INDIVIDUAL TRAINING

AFTER BASIC TRAINING ENDED AT Fort Jackson, I spent a glorious day with the girls, but to be on time for my next reporting, I had to return early on Sunday morning. It was hard to leave them, but I promised them by summertime we would be living on an Army base somewhere, and it would be very exciting.

I took a flight to Baltimore/Washington Airport and a taxi to Aberdeen gate. Not knowing where to go was a problem when I got to Aberdeen. They had probably sent a truck to pick up the new troops from the train station on Friday. At the gate, I asked where my unit was located. Someone gave me a map of the installation, and I set off on foot.

I found the unit's headquarters and a barracks adjacent to it. A female soldier sat outside of the barracks polishing boots. I asked if I was at the right place, and she said yes. I walked into the barracks and looked around, found the girl I had traveled up with, and asked about my gear.

She said she had bad news for me. I thought she had lost my gear or couldn't carry it and left it, but no, this was much, much worse. The platoon sergeant had it in the office, and I was to report to him as soon as I got back. He was not happy.

I thanked the woman, apologized if I got her into any trouble, and walked back out to the company headquarters next door. Here I found a Black staff sergeant with an overly crisp, ironed uniform and mirror finish on his jump boots. He was not as high ranking as our drill sergeants from Fort Jackson, but he certainly outranked my mere E-3 status.

This staff sergeant looked at my name tag and at me, and said, "McNamara! How nice of you to join us! What made you go AWOL, soldier?"

AWOL? I wasn't AWOL, was I? I stayed at attention. I had learned enough in basic that when you are in trouble, stay at attention and let the NCO (noncommissioned officer) ream you a new one because it was going to happen no matter what, and it would only get worse if you opened your mouth or showed any disrespect.

My punishment for this first infraction: cutting grass with a push mower every day after class and all weekend for one month.

"Yes, Sergeant G.," I said, and took my gear and left for the barracks.

After storing my gear and asking, "What did I miss?" I readied myself for the first day of school, then reported back to Sergeant G. for my lawn mower. Training at Aberdeen consisted of purely technical aspects of becoming an Army mechanic. Everything from the use of hand tools and testing equipment to operating a wrecker to pull a truck axle deep in mud was first taught, then practiced, then tested. Each day we took a bus from our barracks to the training facility on the other side of the Chesapeake Bay.

What really surprised me was the number of other women in my squad. I don't remember an exact number, but it was a squad! We had a barracks all to ourselves! Sounds great, right? Well, it wasn't. Remember, the occupants of the barracks have to maintain the barracks. So the ten or so of us had to keep the entire building inspection ready. This had a bit of a negative impact the first week since I also had grass clipping detail every day after training due to my AWOL fiasco. I was one tired troop member by the weekend.

After the first month of grass cutting detail was over, I finally had weekends and evenings to myself. I used the time to do charcoal sketches of the equipment at the outdoor museum which was within walking distance. The museum had various pieces of artillery, tanks, and mortars. I enjoyed putting in the fine details of bolts, threaded artillery tubes, and the broken rubber of the badly worn tank treads. I would send these back to Fort Jackson in a feeble attempt to stay in contact with my old drill sergeant, Sergeant Dugger.

My ploy worked beyond my wildest dreams as I disembarked from the bus after class one Friday to find Drill Sergeant Dugger leaning against a building. I turned my head to the side playfully and smiled from ear to ear with anticipation of a respite from the drudgery of the barracks walls. I quickly double timed to my bunk, changed into civvies, and reported to the orderly room to acquire a pass which would allow me to move freely on and off base for the weekend. Once I had my pass safely tucked into the pocket of my jeans, I ran out to meet him. He held up a finger to slow me, and I slowed to a casual walk the rest of the way to a car which was parked next to the building where he had been patiently waiting.

Once we had exited the main gate I propelled myself across the front seat and wrapped my arms around his neck, planting a hot, wet kiss on the side of his neck. "You're looking good, Mac" he said as he pulled into a motel parking lot down the street and pulled a room key out of his pocket.

Time stood still that weekend. There were fresh fruits and wine in the room. John tempted and teased me with those delicious treats and reminded me once again that under the uniform I was still a woman. As the 48-hour pass ended, we promised to stay in touch, but unfortunately we never did. I am glad he left with such positive memories to cherish.

The weeks passed quickly. The daily lessons and details assigned afterwards kept us so busy that we hardly noticed when we were told that we were halfway through. This was a high point of the training, and we each received a three-day pass and permission to travel off the compound. This time I asked if I could go home. YES! Best news ever!

I quickly packed a few things for the weekend, but then I realized that I had clothes at home. So I put everything back in my locker and headed for the main gate. I caught a taxi, headed to the airport, bought a ticket, and walked into my parents' house before midnight. It was absolutely wonderful to be home. My mom made my favorite chicken casserole for dinner on Saturday night, and we all went down to the lakefront to enjoy the breeze and watch the boats enter and leave the harbor.

My girls would take turns running to the top of a hill in the park and rolling down to the bottom, getting dizzy as they did so. My dad and I sat watching them, catching up on the past five weeks, and I tried to describe Aberdeen Proving Ground to both him and my mom. He was interested in the maintenance skills I had been picking up and said I would be set for life if my car ever broke down! In agreement, I explained it would be easy, since car alternators don't weigh the sixty pounds or more that I had been working on for the last week.

Having something I could share with my dad was really nice. The weekend passed much too quickly, and fearing becoming AWOL again, I actually returned to Aberdeen half a day early. I was sitting on the front porch of the barracks polishing my boots when the others started returning and sharing stories of their break from reality.

Now that we were past the halfway point, we started

thinking and talking about our future. We were getting our first assignments later that week, and the girl who had helped me with my gear on the train, Ginny Lingle, who had also become my roommate, had a boyfriend who was already in the Army at his duty station in Colorado. Ginny was hoping to be stationed with him, but there was no guarantee. Personally, I hoped to be anywhere close to home.

I hadn't researched the locations of Army installations at all, so I had no idea which of them would provide any benefit to a single mom. But when the orders came down, I had Colorado and Ginny had Kansas. "Easy!" I said. "All we have to do is ask them to white out the names and switch!" I was still completely unaware of rules and regulations, I suppose. Our company commander told us that was not how it worked. I felt sorry for Ginny. She looked devastated.

On my visit home the following weekend, I talked to a good friend from high school. I told him what had happened with the assignment, and he let me get my feelings out over a beer at a local bar. His dad, Bob Sr., was also at the bar and Bob went over to talk to him. As they discussed my unfortunate circumstance, the gentleman to the left of Bob's dad joined the conversation.

"You want me to see what I can do, Bob?" asked the greying man.

"Sure! If you have time," Bob Sr. replied, to the man I later learned was our congressional representative, Henry Hyde.

Two days later, when I was returning from class at the end of the day at Aberdeen, my platoon sergeant met me at the bus. This Black man was shaking with rage. He ripped the stripes off of his shirt sleeve and threw them on the dirt in front of me, yelling, "OK, McNamara, you've got my rank and your orders transferred. Are you fucking happy now?"

Oh yes, the shit had hit the fan! Ginny and I were told to report to the company commander. We did, and there and then new sets of orders were issued to us and I was told to stand fast. After Ginny went back to the barracks, I heard about the helicopter that had landed at Aberdeen that morning, how a surprise congressional visit was the one thing no commander relished, how I should have given the commander a heads-up, and how, besides the orders being adjusted "as I had requested," I would also have the privilege of cutting the grass in the company area for the remainder of the time I had at Aberdeen aside from class time.

I returned to the barracks with my new orders and an expectation of blistered fingers in my future. Ginny had no fallout since she had nothing to do with my bringing fire down on our company. I had experience in the grass cutting arena, so I just picked up where I left off several weeks prior. I didn't let it bother me, but I did learn a valuable lesson! If you want something in the military, get your congressperson involved!

I don't remember the graduation ceremony from AIT (Advanced Individual Training). There may have been one. I also don't remember how much time I had to change duty stations. But there was a reasonable amount of time to go home and pack up our belongings, and the girls and I made the move to Fort Riley, Kansas, home of The Big Red One.

8

LITA: THE BIG RED ONE

LOGISTICALLY SPEAKING, THE MOVE TO Kansas was hard. Aside from the changes on a professional level, I had to coordinate myself, my daughters, a home search, and daycare, as well as the typical food, laundry, transportation, and other requirements. These were all new to me.

I didn't have a clue where to go, what to do, or how to do it. The only thing I did know was that the Army didn't wait for you. There was no such thing as being late for work, so I had to figure it all out quickly. Luckily for me, when I first checked in to my unit, I met another mother. This was actually the first I had seen since joining! This woman, Staff Sergeant Jasper, worked in the office at the unit headquarters.

Staff Sergeant Jasper was quite shocked to see that I was not only a mother of two preschool girls, but a single mother of two. She asked me to join her for lunch, and the girls and I did.

As we ate, she quickly filled me in on some details I would need to know. Public transportation: nonexistent between off-post housing and the maintenance shop or anything else on post.

Daycare: reasonable, down the street from the shop. Food and laundry: on the hill. Housing: on post was full, off post had lots of options. As we enjoyed lunch and talked, a very large, muscled Black major walked up and said hi to her, and asked who I was. I stood at attention and gave my name.

"Private McNamara, sir!"

He actually spit out some of what he was drinking as he laughed and said, "Oh? I guess you're new here, Private McNamara. I'm Nate." He held out his hand to shake. Sergeant Jasper told Major Nate Foster that I was a new mechanic in her unit and introduced my girls to him. He smiled at the girls and said hi, to which they all but hid under the table.

The girls were a bit shy, and the newness of everything had them on edge. I quickly explained that I was a private and couldn't call an officer by their first name. Noticing his name tape on the front of his uniform as "Foster," I finished with "Major Foster, sir."

He laughed again. "OK, Mac." And the nickname was permanently mine. Major Foster asked where I was living.

I answered with "A motel just off base."

He asked how I was getting around.

I told him by taxi.

"OK, let's get you set up, Mac," he said.

Sergeant Jasper smiled and said this was a good thing.

Nate was a property owner who rented to many soldier's families. He was also a World Class Powerlifter and not too bad on the eyes. I was relieved and really felt very at ease with this total stranger with the warm smile and bulging muscles. He asked Sergeant Jasper if she was finished with me (she was), and he asked if I wanted to go check out some rental units (I did), and we were off!

It turned out that Major Foster owned a dozen or so mobile homes that he rented out to soldiers from Fort Riley. He showed me a couple in a mobile home park very near the front gate, easy to get to and from the Fort by taxi, and then one far from the Fort at the edge of a cornfield. Across the street from the field was a residential neighborhood with a playground.

"Kathy, I mean, Staff Sergeant Jasper, lives down the street. You might be able to hop a ride to the Fort with her until you get some wheels."

I must have looked like I really liked this option better. "Hang on a minute," he said. He drove to the end of the block and called out to a man cutting grass. The two talked for a bit. The man went into the house and then returned in a few minutes, speaking again with Major Foster before he returned to the car, again with a huge grin.

"She said she would be happy to! What do you think? You want to look inside?" He held out some keys as he cocked his head in the direction of the cornfield and trailer home up the street. I smiled in return and said, "Yes! Thank you, sir!"

He smiled again and said, "It really is Nate."

I only smiled and shook my head.

The trailer was wonderful. It came fully furnished and was what they called a double-wide. It was two trailer widths put together and looked more like a house. It had more bedrooms than we needed, a nice sized kitchen, living room, two bathrooms, and a small porch in the front facing the street. I had an idea of rental costs from the Chicago suburbs but no idea how much things cost here. I was pleasantly shocked when he explained it was within my ability to pay. I gladly said I would sign the lease. And with that, my girls and I had a home!

Nate drove us back to Fort Riley and dropped us off with Sergeant Jasper once more.

"We're going to be neighbors!" she said, with a genuine smile.

"Yes, I am so happy to have run into Major Foster like that," I replied.

"I may have had something to do with that," she said with a

wink. "I called him and let him know you were looking and where we were having lunch. Nate's a very good man. He has a young son. He knows what it's like to be a single parent in the Army. He likes to help when he can."

Her words amazed me, and I shook my head in the realization that I had just been accepted into the Army family. After her shift ended, Kathy drove us down the hill and we stopped at the daycare facility to pick up her daughter. She introduced me to the head of the facility and I filled out the paperwork so Jean and Kymberly could attend the next week.

Kathy then drove us all home, stopping at the motel so I could get our clothes on the way. With that whirlwind of a day, I felt a new order to my life. It wasn't quite the order I had during basic or AIT, but it was order nonetheless, and it really did feel good. We were invited to have dinner with Kathy, her husband, and their daughter. Afterward, the girls all played at the park down the street and Kathy and I sat watching them as we discussed plans for the rest of the weekend.

Kathy took us shopping for food the next morning, and I spent the rest of the weekend putting clothes away and setting up the kitchen with the newly purchased groceries and freshly washed dishes. I had rewashed everything in the trailer, not knowing how clean the previous tenants were.

Kathy brought down a basket of toys for my girls, along with her daughter, who was, to our amusement, happy to explain how the toys worked.

The weekend passed quickly and before we knew it, it was 0400 hours on Monday, time to leave for Fort Riley and my new career. We stopped briefly at the daycare facility to drop off our charges and then drove up the street a block and a half to where other soldiers were already forming up for PT.

PT started at 0500 following roll call. It was here that I was introduced to the platoon sergeant, Sergeant First Class Bobby

Adams. He towered over every person in the platoon by at least a foot. He had a laid-back attitude, but you still got the feeling that he was all business, and that no nonsense would be allowed. Following roll call, we took off running as a group down the middle of the street, singing cadence as we went.

Following the morning run, we realigned into formation and then were dismissed to start the workday. I was instructed to report to the office, a glassed-off work area adjacent to the work bays where trucks were parked in various stages of disassembly. As I approached the office doors, I quickly noticed that all of the women, including Kathy, were inside the glass enclosure, and Sergeant Adams was leaning on a desk talking with a warrant officer.

I entered and reported to the warrant officer, snapping to attention. Sergeant Adams smiled and said, "You gotta love the newbies."

The warrant officer returned my salute and told me to be "at ease," which I did, still within regulation. "Have a seat, Mac," the warrant officer said, pointing to a desk behind me.

"Sir?" I said.

"Have a seat," he said again. "That will be your desk."

I stood, possibly too long.

Sergeant Adams said in a stern voice, "You heard the order?"

I stumbled over my words, speaking to both men simultaneously. "Sir, Sergeant, I am a 63H. I am reporting for duty as a mechanic, sir, Sergeant." I was not really sure who I was supposed to be responding to.

The warrant officer spoke to me directly. "Private McNamara, this is the office section of the maintenance shop where we assign work orders and track parts usage and man hours. You can use that typewriter at that desk." He stopped, no doubt thinking that he had made himself much clearer now.

"But, sir, I don't know how to type, and I trained to be a

mechanic. I am prepared to do that. But, sir, I am not an office worker." I waited, thinking this is where I would be given the task of cutting grass.

"OK," the warrant officer said. "Give Private McNamara a toolbox." He glanced at the work schedule board on the wall. "Bryant and Wooten, office," he called into a microphone on his desk. "McNamara, you will work with Bryant and Wooten. Dismissed."

I saluted and said, "Yes, sir," turned and saw the other two soldiers walking into the office.

"Bryant, Wooten, you're with McNamara here. Show her the tool room," the warrant officer said.

"Yes, sir," they replied, and we departed the office.

Bryant and Wooten were the soldiers' last names. Everyone was called by their last name, albeit usually with a rank in front. Private McNamara was mine. Many people had nicknames as well. Mine was always "Mac."

Wooten was a tall, gangly private from North Carolina. He was very low key and relaxed; nothing ever bothered him. Bryant, from South Carolina, was his opposite as he was short in stature and temper! I liked them both, and we made a good team.

Three other aspects of my Fort Riley duty station are worth mentioning: 1) Being a female mechanic had its challenges. 2) I was still a soldier and a mom. 3) My ex-husband could continue to foul up my career path and life.

I was happy to have a toolbox and a team to train with and actual equipment to work on. Our duties usually consisted of transmission or transfer cases R&R (repair and replace) on two-and-a-half or five-ton trucks. These pieces of equipment were massive in size and weight. It took a hoist overhead with a come-along and a jack underneath to remove and replace the 250-pound-gear-filled unit. Typically, we worked as a team, and since I was the newbie, I usually had the least exciting tasks.

I did watch and continued to learn, but I spent a lot of the first few months fetching tools and small parts and cleaning parts and the work bay after hours.

One particular day we were replacing a transmission and I was perched in the truck cab, where the driver and passenger would sit. I had the "dog house" (a metal plate covering the top of the transmission) removed and placed aside. A chain sling or come-along was affixed to the front top and rear of the new transmission with bolts, and the sling was suspended on a hydraulic hoist that Wooten was operating from his position on the garage floor next to the truck. Bryant had the uncomfortable position of being on his back underneath the transmission.

There was no jack in place since we were replacing it and all we needed to do was swing it into position and bolt it up. Bryant was grunting and swearing under the truck. He was obviously having an issue lining the transmission case within the engine. I could see him using his boots and kicking it several times. I had already done my part and was just sitting, waiting for my next task, which would be to crank the come-along with a ratchet to balance the trans as it went in.

I looked up to see the platoon sergeant standing next to the open cab door with his hands on his hips in a bit of a rage. "What happened to Bryant?" he asked, rather coarsely. I glanced down at the floor under the truck. No Bryant.

"I don't know, Sergeant. Maybe he went to get a pry bar? He was having trouble getting the trans lined up," I said.

"No, dammit! What happened? How did he get hurt? Where are his fingers? They need those fingers!" he replied.

My mouth fell open. I looked over to where Wooten had been standing, but he was now gone, as was Bryant. *What the heck just happened? How did I not notice this?* "I don't know, Sergeant," was all I could say.

"Well, get down there and look for those fingers, Mac, and do it quick!" With that, I finally recovered from my initial shock and quickly clambered out of the truck and slid underneath where Bryant had been working. I lay on the floor first looking around on the ground. Finger? No, bolt. I then imagined him lying there kicking the trans. He would have had to balance himself somehow to put any pressure onto the casing with his feet.

I automatically reached my hands up to grasp the crossmember where the bottom of the trans was sitting. There on the crossmember were Bryant's fingers. I shook off the sudden feeling of nausea, took them off of the metal beam, and crawled out from under the truck.

"You got them?" the platoon sergeant asked.

"Yes, Sergeant," I replied, and he instructed me to get in the jeep that was running at the front of the garage. He hopped in the driver's seat as I hopped into the passenger seat, and we were off on a fast pace up the hill to the hospital on base. We rushed to the emergency room, which was easy to find by the red cross on the wall and Bryant's screams of pure agony.

I stopped running only when I reached the room where he was crying out in pain and held out my hand to the medic who stood in the room. As I handed over the greasy, smashed fingers, I stared at my buddy, his hand immersed in a jar of clear liquid. I guessed it was an antiseptic but not analgesic. The tears flowed down his face, and Wooten, who was behind him, supported his back as they both tried to stay upright.

The mangled stubs of Bryant's hand may never grasp a ratchet again, I thought. My thoughts turned into words and I asked the medic, "Can you sew them back on?" The medic looked at the filthy, smashed, now-drying digits I had given him.

"I don't know. We'll see."

The words that we said to each other, however, triggered Bryant to stop screaming. Just like that, he stopped. He sniffled a little, wiped his face with the sleeve of his other arm, and said,

"Thanks, Mac."

The doctors were unable to save all of the fingers. Only one was salvageable. He was left with his thumb and part of one finger to oppose it. He spent the next three months on light duty and worked in the tool room signing out equipment. From there, he was probably given a discharge. I don't know, since by the time his light duty was up, I had been discharged and was on my way home.

9

LITA: GOING, A GHOST, A GUY, AND GONE

AS YOU CAN SEE, I assimilated well into my new life as a mechanic. Besides working on the Army equipment, I found that the guys in my platoon also worked on their own vehicles in their time off. I was one of the only platoon members who lived off post. Almost everyone else lived in the barracks. Since I was much older than my peers, and had a rental trailer, without the restrictions of barracks life, my place was often used for weekend get-togethers. It was the place for barbecues, assorted under the hood work on everyone's cars, and for just destressing after a hard week at work.

This was when I purchased my first car. I bought a 1965 Ford Galaxie 500 with a blown engine for a hundred dollars from one of the guys in the unit. He said he was done trying to fix it at the post, where there were restrictions on leaving a vehicle in inoperable condition for any length of time. He had gotten numerous tickets for the white smoke pouring out of the tailpipe, so I got a deal I couldn't pass up!

I decided to rebuild the motor of my 1965 Ford Galaxie 500.

It had a 390 cubic inch engine. The guys brought over an engine hoist. We hauled it out and placed it on an old tire next to my trailer. I tore it down and replaced the pistons, rings, bearings, and oil pump. I bought new heads and put it all back together with a new gasket set during the week after work.

At this point in my girls' lives, they got their first taste of "mom the mechanic." I brought the smaller pieces inside the trailer, and we worked together on cleaning and polishing them till they looked new again. They did play outside with other kids their age as well, but I had enjoyed being a part of household repairs with my dad growing up and hoped the experience could somehow bring my girls and me closer together as well.

Two weeks later, the finished motor was ready to be reinstalled. This went rather smoothly in between burgers grilling and beers on ice. A group of six or more from my platoon were over to help since I had never done this in a small vehicle.

Once the engine was bolted up and cranked over, I excitedly wanted to take it for a spin. I was warned that I needed to do a proper engine break-in with varying speeds and loads. I did as instructed, and once the rings were seated, the oil pressure was up to par, and the coolant stayed at a respectable 185 degrees, I took her on the highway. I enjoyed the feeling of the powerful engine pulling this 3,800-pound girl! I kept thinking about how smooth the performance was with a naturally aspirated four-barrel Holley carb under the hood.

I glanced down to see how fast I could get her to go and saw the speedometer wasn't working. *Damn! I'll have to get that fixed ASAP.* But I really wanted to know what she could do, so I continued. Just then I saw flashing lights in my rearview mirror. *Well, now I guess I will find out.*

I pulled the car to the shoulder and let the engine return to a quiet methodical hum. The officer walked up and asked, "Do you know how fast you were going?"

I honestly replied, "No," and made the mistake of adding, "How fast was I going?" with possibly too much glee in my voice.

"One hundred and ten miles per hour," he responded, to which I let out a "HOOOAH!" Again, unneeded commentary from me.

He gave me a quizzical look, so I readily explained that this was my very first project car and I was really proud of the work I had done. I immediately apologized and changed my tone to fit the situation, stating I really did abide by the laws and that he would see that I had never received a ticket.

The officer asked me why I didn't know how fast I had been going, and I admitted that I must have had a bad speedometer or that I had forgotten to hook it up during the install. That was the worst thing I guess I could have said. We then commenced with a vehicle safety check. Wipers? No, not hooked up. Turn signals? Not yet. Headlights? No, sir. Horn? Hmmmm, no. Reverse lights? Not sure—we can hope? No. That added up to seven tickets. That was going to hurt!

As you can tell, my next weekend off was spent putting the car into compliance with the laws of the state of Kansas, leaving only the speeding ticket. Talk about a painful lesson I would never repeat!

On the more personal side of my life at Fort Riley, I started dating a man in my platoon. He was the squad leader, an E-5. He was probably five years my senior, from Mississippi, and was separated with two boys of his own.

He and I felt very different when we were together. We weren't soldiers and friends like the rest of my platoon. We were a mom and dad with children to care for, and the Army was just the job we went to work for every day. The attachment was strong, and I felt I could easily spend the rest of my life raising a slightly larger family with Ed Leonard.

I knew, however, that I would have to take my time breaking the news to those at home. Ed was Black, and although we were not raised with any overt prejudice I was aware of, I would be the first in the family to become seriously involved with someone not Caucasian.

Ed's children were a little older than my girls as well, and were enrolled in kindergarten and first grade at a school up on the hill. My two were in preschool on the main fort, down the street from our maintenance shop. Jean was four, and Kym was three. Every morning, I would drop them off at preschool then continue up the road to our shop. Our platoon met in the back of the building and did a poor example of PT (some jumping jacks and push-ups) before reporting to the shop office for our assignments.

I think we didn't do PT because our platoon sergeant was a heavy drinker. He talked about hard liquor like it was the only thing there was to drink. Now that I know a bit more about cirrhosis, I might venture a guess that his liver was already failing at that point. At any rate, if we wanted to pass our PT test, we had to train on our own.

One afternoon, while test driving a deuce and a half, I spotted a young boy, maybe two years old, walking in the grass. I stopped the truck, looked around, and found that he was alone. Being across the street from the daycare facility, I assumed he had come from there. At first I was happy to have found him safe, but I quickly began to feel a rage that this facility could lose a little boy! If I brought him back in their front door, the entire situation might be swept under the rug with no remediation taken to ensure that it didn't happen again.

I left my truck on the road, switched it off, picked the little boy up, and carried him up the road to the shop. I yelled inside to Ed that I had to take care of something personal, and that he needed to go get my truck. I then put the little guy in the back seat of my car and drove up the hill to the commanding general's office. I told the officer at the reception desk that I had to speak with the general, that it was a critical safety issue.

Having an open-door policy allowed even E-3s to request permission to talk to the commander. You always had to go through the chain of command first, however. In this case, I figured safety trumped the chain of command. The officer who manned the reception desk allowed us into the office, and the commander stood and walked forward to greet my little friend and me.

I apologized for the intrusion but explained I also had children at the daycare facility and feared if I didn't bring the situation to the attention of someone responsible, it might not be addressed. Safety was my concern, and I knew that it was the commander's responsibility.

He thanked me, agreed with me, called his assistant back into the office, and dismissed me as he reached down to pick up the little boy and held him on his lap. Then I heard him begin to explain to the other officer what I had just brought to his attention. I felt good driving back down the hill. I felt confident that the children would be better cared for from that day forward.

There was a bit more excitement in our day-to-day lives as we spent the next year in Kansas. The trailers where we lived were tightly packed, and the children in the neighborhood often just spent time running between trailers playing hide and seek.

For a few months, I had a roommate, another girl in our company. She wanted to get out of the barracks but couldn't afford to get her own place. I had an extra bedroom in my trailer, so I rented it to her. It was a win-win, until one night when she got out of bed angry that she couldn't sleep with all of the banging noises outside. *What banging noise?* I wondered. I didn't hear anything.

She insisted that someone, maybe a kid, was playing around outside and banging on the side of the trailer under her window. We all needed sleep, so I got dressed and went out to look for the raucous scamps. I saw no one and came inside.

I told the girl that the kid had obviously moved on, but she said, "No, they are doing it again!"

I was still at the doorway, so I poked my head outside and said, "Nope," to which she insisted the noise was continuing. I walked through the living room to her room, the first one on the left. I walked in and suddenly, I could also hear the banging! I looked at her and said, "But I could swear there was no one there!"

The girl went out to check for herself. Without walking outside in her pajamas, she simply leaned out of the doorway to look down the length of the trailer. "OK," she said, "No one is here." I heard her, but I also could still hear the banging on the wall. It wasn't the tinny fiberglass sound you might expect from someone hitting the side of a fiberglass trailer. It was a deeper hollow sound and as we both walked up to the wall to investigate, the sound stopped. Not knowing what to think of it, we just shrugged and went back to sleep.

Over the next few weeks, the noises continued. My girls had gone home to spend the mandatory two weeks of visitation with their father, so it was just my roommate and me. When the cabinet doors started opening and closing on their own, we both began thinking out loud, "Is this place haunted?"

One night, my roommate ran out of her bedroom soaked in sweat, yelling that she felt a cold, heavy presence. She insisted that it was a ghost and that it had settled on her chest as she was lying in bed. I tried everything to calm her down.

I told her, "Ghosts do not exist. You were probably dreaming. You're catching a cold." Nothing I said would convince her to stay. She was already packing her clothes into her car, and had moved out in less than an hour. The concern over the "ghost" didn't bother me at all; it was more the sudden loss of rent. I remember thinking that I myself would have to move at the end of the month to a smaller trailer.

While the girls were still in Chicago, things became much more eventful at the trailer. The noises continued. The cabinets kept opening and closing without reason. One day, as I was lying on the couch watching TV, the refrigerator opened!

That's a heavy door, I thought. *How could house settling, or any other such excuse I've come up with for these episodes, actually open a refrigerator door? Did I not close it properly? That has to be it.* I got up and walked to the open door. The coolness that emitted from the opening suddenly blasted like a strong northeast wind barreling down the Great Lakes.

It was an active force, not the ambient coolness that should have slowly dropped to the floor from the appliance. I stood frozen from fear, not from the actual temperature drop. I shook slightly but regained my strength and composure, reaching into the still-open doorway to grab a bottle of water. I closed the door solidly, making sure there was no question about its security.

I returned to the couch and resumed my post of relaxing in front of the television. Before I could open my bottle, however, I felt a large pressure on my chest. I also saw a dark shadow hovering over me. I immediately closed my eyes. I told myself it was an illusion, a side effect of a heart attack, anything but a ghost! I opened my eyes, and the shadow was gone.

That night, I slept in the spare room since I had already started packing up my room for the move in a few weeks to a less expensive trailer. As I was falling asleep, I heard the noises from the wall behind the headboard of the bed. I ignored them. I could actually sleep through any noise. I think I got that from basic training, where you slept any time you had five minutes to spare.

As I slept, I had a bothersome dream. I don't know what it was about but I know I woke up in a sweat and sat upright in bed in a frightened state. I saw the same shadow in a standing position, in the fuzzy figure of a man, but just a shadow. Seriously! Yes, I may have been dreaming. I looked at the shadow and started praying.

I went through the whole rosary before it departed. It disappeared. Poof! Gone! I was still sweating, still praying, still staring at the spot where the shadow had been. Was it a dream?

I didn't know. The girls came back the following week and as we were packing up their things for the move, they asked an odd question. "Should we leave some toys for the ghost?"

Shocked, I asked, "What?"

Jean explained that a ghost would play with their toys at night, moving them around and lifting them in the air.

You might be thinking I am off my rocker. I am not trying to prove or disprove an oddity like this, just mentioning what happened. I think very scientifically and try to reason things out with proven facts as a measure. But these events happened, and I can't explain them, so they will remain unexplained.

I ended my initial active duty stint a year after arriving at The Big Red One. My ex-husband had again changed his mind about my choice to be a member of the military and took me back to court demanding weekend visitation with Jean and Kym. With my current job, there was no reasonable way to transport them to and fro.

At the same time, the Army made me sign an agreement stating that I had emergency childcare available for the girls in case of deployment. They also gave me the option to take an honorable discharge if I was not deployable. I took the discharge and returned home in April 1979. I felt disheartened and lost. How was I to support my children? What would become of us now?

10

LITA: AIR FORCE AFTER ALL

ARRIVING HOME, ONCE AGAIN UNEMPLOYED, I once again moved in with my parents for a short time. My mom was always willing to care for the girls as I worked small part-time positions and hunted for something that paid well.

My family and I noticed that Jean Marie, now four years old, was having some medical problems: chronic urinary tract infections that lasted for months. This was rather odd for a child so young, but it took me a while to put it together. I didn't think much of it, but now that I was home I began to look at everything with suspicion. *Could her father be touching her inappropriately during their time together?* I wondered. I did not know what to do next. My parents agreed that the best thing to do would be to take him back to court and stop visitation.

I found an apartment I could afford, and hired a new lawyer. My daughter had testing done to determine if the infections could have come from such a horrible event, and I took her to see a child psychologist.

All of my fears had come true, and I felt like a failure as a mother for not being able to keep my girls safe from the same predator who had first accosted me when I was a teenager.

This court battle would last for years, with supervised visitations still approved until I finally got the court's approval to have sole custody with no further visitation. The damage, of course, was done by this time, causing emotional scars that will probably haunt us forever.

During the first two years of this court proceeding, I was no longer in the military. I took work in the civilian sector, building diesel engines until International Harvester went on a six-month strike. I then moved back to diesel mechanics at the Chicago Transit Authority and a suburban transit system. I also attended Triton Community College, in River Grove, Illinois at night, earning an associate's degree.

Missing the structure and camaraderie of the military, I went to a local recruiter and searched for solutions. I explained where I had been and where I wanted to go. I had recently received an associate's of science degree in diesel mechanics and was thinking that an engineering future might be a good idea.

The recruiter searched the resources available. He found an Air Force Reserve unit at our local airport that had openings for engineer techs with on-the-job training (OJT). I jumped at the idea of being part of the military once again, still living at home and continuing my career field advancement. The unit was close enough to home, so I could spend quality time with my girls and it could lead to a job in aviation. I was again excited about the future and what it might hold.

The 928th was located at O'Hare, a half hour from my house on good traffic days. Not until I had once again committed to the program did I learn that they were a civil engineering unit. Their wartime mission was rapid runway repair. This had nothing at all to do with mechanical engineering, which was what I had wanted to do.

My new military career would be as a site developer, and my new toolbox had a transit and a pole. I was responsible for marking the ground elevation wherever the unit was working. This also allowed me to work more active duty time for training in various bases around the country.

This position took me to Pennsylvania to help with the installation of a new sidewalk between two barracks; to Florida, where we actually blew up an unused runway just to patch it again, and to Georgia to assist on an office building remodel at Warner Robins Air Force Base. It was here that I met a lovely Southern lady by the name of Ann Miles. She had been working as a civilian in the building we were assigned to overhaul.

Ann and I instantly became friends, and I spent a great deal of my off-duty time with her and her son. This assignment was six weeks long. As a member of the 928th, you could do the first two weeks, the middle two weeks, the last two weeks, or any configuration between them. I was currently between jobs and not dating anyone at the time, so I opted to stay all six weeks.

When I first arrived at the air base, I asked an active duty member working the desk at the terminal about ground transportation. The member advised me that the motor pool was across the street, which was where reservists usually signed out vehicles.

I walked across the street, walked up to the desk clerk at the motor pool, and inquired about a set of wheels. He asked what unit I was with and how long the assignment orders were.

I replied, and he had me sign the typical equipment release form and told me where to find the jeep. I was feeling pretty good about the Air Force. We didn't get this kind of service in the Army!

I checked into the barracks that would be my home for the next six weeks and then went back to check out the base and grab a bite to eat. I saw a friend coming out of the men's quarters and asked if he wanted to come along. He hopped in the passenger seat and off we went.

DeWayne Reynolds was an E-6 and had a few more than I did in the military and on earth. His hair was platinum grey, but he had a full head of it and with his tanned, chiseled face, he was nice to look at! He immediately asked where I got the vehicle. I explained I had gotten it from the motor pool, and he just cocked his head slightly like he was trying to figure that out. Then he shrugged and said, "Great! Where are you taking me, sweetheart?" *This might turn out to be the best annual training session ever!* I thought.

After we grabbed lunch and drove around the base a little bit to get our bearings, we headed back to our quarters. As soon as we arrived, I noticed a small group of other airmen gathered in a huddle at the intersection where the barracks and the mess hall met. It was easy to see that our unit commander had arrived. At six foot seven, he towered over everyone else in the unit.

I parked the vehicle, and DeWayne and I walked up to the group. Even though it was an informal gathering, we both approached the officer and saluted and greeted him by his rank of colonel. The commander returned our salute and looked straight at me. "So, Mac, I hear you volunteered as my driver? Good! Let's get my gear loaded up so I can go get settled in. You were out doing a recon? You know where the BOQ is?"

The BOQ, or base officer quarters, was a few blocks away. We had passed them on our drive, and yes, as you have probably surmised, I had signed out our commander's vehicle, the only one the motor pool had available. The six weeks passed quickly, and I was happy to be back home with my girls, now ages seven and eight.

The next annual training would turn out to be more enjoyable than any other. We received an assignment to install a fire hydrant system at a NATO base on the island of Crete off the southern tip of Greece! Because of the distance we would travel, and the estimated time to actually start the project, we were on twenty-one-day orders. *This is the chance of a lifetime,* I thought.

I decided I would figure out a way to bring my girls with me this time. I just had to figure out the logistics. I immediately thought of my new friend from Georgia. Ann Miles had a young son a bit older than my girls. A full-time government worker with years in the system, I knew she would have the leave time available. The phone call was full of excitement—"GREECE?!" She was on board immediately and more than happy to play nanny to my two while I was working and for the travel portion of the trip.

I had to fly with my unit in a C-130 with sling net seats and a curtain enclosed latrine an arm's length from the seating area. Meals consisted of bagged sandwiches and fruit. We had soft drinks or water in a cooler secured to the luggage pallet. Our luggage consisted of duffle bags, all piled on a pallet at the tail end of a cavernous, cold, and noisy plane.

We used our earplugs from the range to keep the noise level to a manageable drone. Field jackets with liners and leather gloves with wool liners helped somewhat with the cold. We couldn't have gotten hypothermia—it wasn't that cold—but it was extremely hard to get used to the temperature during the seventeen-hour flight! And did I mention the pain?

I had developed appendicitis in the weeks leading up to the trip. It was chronic, not acute, and I was being treated with antibiotics. The inflamed organ made sitting in the soft web seating that much harder. My abdomen was contorted into a pretzel with the lack of a firm seat or back. Once my squad learned about the reason for my discomfort, they started taking bets on who would be able to remove my appendix with their government-issued pocket knives during the flight if it came down to it.

My task on the island of Crete, Greece, was to set the first ever benchmark for construction crews to use on the NATO Air Base at Heraklion. When construction projects are done, an engineer uses a benchmark (distance above sea level) to add or subtract soil. Allowing for proper drainage, etc., this benchmark starts with sea level. The appropriate sea level is measured over time to average in factors of tide, which change with the cycles of the moon.

Exciting as it sounds, I had to stand in the Sea of Crete a few feet off shore and hold my leveling rod while another member of my squad used a transit to measure the vertical datum. This level would eventually be moved uphill to the NATO base. Once my measurement was taken, I was assigned to assist the wing commander in designing a golf course for the MWR, the Morale, Welfare, and Recreation section of the base.

Every day at three, Ann and the kids picked me up at the front gate, and we drove to a nearby restaurant for dinner. The time went fast. We had a three-day pass in the middle of the assignment. Some of my unit chose to fly to Egypt. Ann, the kids, and I decided to go to the mainland and tour Athens.

As I traveled with the service, I would often wonder what to bring home to my girls as an inexpensive souvenir so they would know where I was when I wasn't at home with them and that I was thinking of them. I chose geology and would bring them each a rock native to the region. They received limestone from Kansas, sand and clay from South Carolina, and crystalline igneous rock from Maryland.

I guess this is what Jean was thinking of as we toured the ruins of the Greek Acropolis. Half way through our guided tour she handed me her sweater, all bunched up in a ball and said, "Mom, can you carry my sweater? It's heavy."

I took the sweater, surprised at the obvious weight to it, and looked more closely at the bundle. Shocked, I stopped dead in my tracks and pulled her aside, "Jean, what are these?" I tried to ask without sounding too upset.

It turned out she had been collecting pieces of the different monuments and ruins since we arrived at the mainland in Athens. There were dozens of varied sized chunks of delicately carved marble, granite, and limestone. She explained they were rocks from the trip to save for the future so we would remember where we had been.

I caught up with the tour where Ann, her son, and Kym were waiting for us, explaining to Ann that we had a problem. She looked and laughed so hard that the tour participants must have wondered what was going on with the U.S. visitors.

We decided since we didn't know where each piece came from, we would just keep them, but I advised the girls we couldn't do that type of thing when visiting ancient sites like these.

I guess it was a good reminder to myself as well, because the next week, we visited the Palace of Knossos on Crete, an ancient Minoan structure from approximately 1300 B.C., excavated in the 20th century. The palace had layers of wallpaper in the Queen's chamber, and I badly wanted to tear off a chunk to bring home to show my mom, as she claimed the title of wallpaper-whisperer of the 1960s and 70s. But I respected the sage advice I had given the girls, and kept my hands in my pockets.

Ann and I tried to make the trip as educational as possible for the children, and I am told they all remember it to this day.

Once we arrived back in the States my appendix was removed, and I felt much better physically. I also began thinking long and hard about my future in the military. The Air Force was fun, exciting, and a completely different type of military service than the Army. When going to the field, the Army put up small two-person tents you had to crawl in and out of. The Air Force put us up in hotel rooms.

Food was so much better in the Air Force, too. We actually had lobster tail and steak for special occasions! The Army holiday meal might be turkey with potatoes. So my Air Force squad mates all thought I had lost my mind when I told them I was going back to the Army. The problem was that I really wanted to become an officer. The Air Force had a four-year college requirement. I only had a two-year degree. There was also a maximum age to become an officer—thirty-two and a half at the time of commissioning.

I was already an old fart of thirty-one years. I couldn't see how I could possibly add to my civilian education and complete the military training to become an officer without going back to the Army. After weighing the possibilities, I chose the Illinois Army National Guard as my next assignment. They had a state Officer Candidate School (OCS). The OCS program lasted eighteen months and the training took place in Springfield, Illinois. That was about a three-hour drive each way. I was determined to make it work.

Once I made the transition to the National Guard, I wouldn't have access to the extra duty weeks or months that I enjoyed in the Air Force Reserves. Those extra duty assignments helped in more ways than adding to my retirement points, as I also received extra pay, including travel pay. This helped enormously, since I was otherwise unemployed.

Considering my change in circumstances, I started scanning the papers for employment that wouldn't take me away from my duties as a single mom, would pay enough to allow us to finally move out on our own, and would not interfere with my weekend requirements at the National Guard. A tall order, apparently.

But one interesting ad caught my attention. It asked for "a personal attendant to assist men and women with various needs." I called the number and a woman with a southern drawl answered the phone. She was extremely vague on the phone, but suggested we meet in an hour at a tollway rest stop not far from my home. I assumed she was traveling and wanted to do a quick interview before she left town for the weekend. I agreed and headed for I-294 and the Hillside toll plaza.

I described myself to her when we spoke, and I guess I did a decent job in doing so, since she walked up to me as I entered the plaza, introduced herself, and made sure I was who she expected. We grabbed a coffee and sat at a table overlooking the traffic whizzing by below us.

She was about ten years older than I was, with platinum blond hair and large bones. Standing at about five feet nine inches, she had heavily lined hands, as if she worked outdoors for a number of years. Not knowing anything about the position, I waited to see what she had to say. She didn't have any application forms or company brochures with her, so I assumed it was simply an initial meet and greet. She started out by asking about me.

I explained I was a single mom, and about my upcoming position in the National Guard. I told her I was trained as a mechanic, but was looking for something that didn't include weekends, since I didn't know what my Guard schedule would look like for the next few years.

She said the schedule could be flexible.

I asked if the individuals needing help were in private homes or nursing care facilities, and she laughed so hard that I think we drew attention from everyone in the rest stop!

"Oh my!" she said, in her strong Southern accent. "Do you not know what this is about?"

I must have blushed and said, "No, I guess not," at which point she stood up to leave. I immediately jumped to my feet and grabbed her arm as she turned to leave.

She turned toward me and said, "It's okay, I don't mean you any ill-will, but if you don't know which ad you were replying to, I think it's best that we forget about the offer."

I don't know why, but I asked her to please stay, and explained I was interested, I just didn't understand.

She looked around to see if anyone was watching, and then sat down again. "Lita," she said frankly, "I run an elite service for men and women who have trouble in the bedroom."

Now, I know I blushed, but I didn't hesitate. I said I would like to know more. After talking for the next half hour or so, I learned about an industry that I had not been introduced to previously. This woman owned a call girl service that matched elite clients with women who could satisfy their various needs.

My initial concerns were safety, legality, hours, and pay. She made a quick phone call and a man walked over from a table on the other end of the plaza. She introduced him as her husband, and explained girls never went out alone. Her husband or another bodyguard would accompany me to each appointment. I could use someone of my choosing if I wanted, and if I did, I wouldn't have to pay the surcharge for the service they already had in place.

I asked about the hours and the pay. The hours were entirely up to me. She could easily see me working as many hours as I wanted. Legality was the area that I should have spent more time thinking about, but when she said I would make $500 an hour, I think rational thinking left my mind faster than the cars below us.

She had a few requirements I hadn't expected when I walked into the interview, but in retrospect, they made perfect sense. I was always to dress in business dresses or a suit with a skirt and jacket, and always to wear three-inch heels. I hesitated when she said that, and she immediately added that she would take me shopping and pay for my first three sets of clothes.

I was convinced. We shook hands, and I left the plaza for my car, which was parked on the northbound exit. She exited the opposite side, heading south. I should have taken the I-290 interchange towards Oak Park five miles up the road, but I was lost in thought, and continued driving north passing O'Hare Airport, where I had recently been assigned as a reservist. I quickly got my bearings, flipped around at the O'Hare interchange, and headed back home. It was still early, and I had to pass Northlake on the way home, so I stopped by to see DeWayne to get his opinion on the idea.

He was massively excited over the whole thing, which surprised me a bit. I thought he might have felt hurt, but he said he supported the idea, and would be my chauffeur/ bodyguard if I wanted. I explained that he would be paid $50 an hour, and that sealed the deal. From that day until my arrest about a year later, I was a call girl for one of the most exclusive agencies in Chicago.

I insisted on staying true to the ad that I responded to: my goal was to assist men and women who were having trouble interacting with others. My clients included young people with emotional or mental disabilities, individuals with gender dysphoria, or women who believed they were lesbians but weren't sure how to act naturally during their first time. Although I don't remember all of the clients I worked with, I can tell you a little bit about three whom I remember vividly.

The first was a Vietnam veteran who had severe PTSD and refused to leave his home. He lived as a recluse and wanted someone to talk with and nothing else. I had difficulty leaving at the end of each hour visit and found it difficult to take his money. I felt he needed more than what I could possibly provide, but he refused any suggestions I made for him to try and get help through the VA. He was a regular who would book me every month, and he asked for me specifically when he called to make an appointment.

The second was a rather young man. I believe he was on the Autism spectrum. He did not want to engage in sex at all, but wanted to wrestle on the floor while we were both in our underwear. He was also a regular, and I knew I would be sore after meeting with him, since I was not much of a wrestler! I would make sure I didn't have any other clients the day or so after meeting with him.

The last client I recall well was a large, hulking Black man who towered over me by at least a foot. At first, I was wary and unsure of the safety of working with him, as his sheer size was intimidating. Once we sat down to talk, however, I felt very much at ease, and when he undressed to show his lacy bra and panties, I understood why he used our service.

I had no problem with his clothing choice, other than realizing that it was of much better quality than what I was wearing! He did require sex, but limited our activities to oral. I was able to stay completely dressed. I later found out from another girl who worked in our agency that he was a pro football player.

The job came to an abrupt halt when I was called to a hotel room in downtown Chicago. I felt uneasy with the entire call. I had not been accustomed to meeting men at hotels. This was a first. My bodyguard would be circling the block outside, which made me feel very uneasy as well, and I had never met with this person before. I was tempted to turn down the call and let someone else take it, but he guaranteed a three-hour service call, which sounded like a good piece of change to end the week.

I knocked on the door of the hotel room I was instructed to go to, and was greeted by a man in a business suit. He asked if I was from the agency, and I said I was. He welcomed me and stepped over to the table near the windows and took a seat. That movement made me feel a little more at ease, and I entered the room, closing the door behind me. I went to the table and sat next to him, taking a bottle of water that was on the minibar on my way over. As I sat down, he asked, "What is the charge?"

I responded by saying the rate should have been explained over the phone when he made the appointment.

He said he forgot what it was exactly, so I said $500 an hour and that he had booked a three-hour session, so $1,500. He reached into his pocket for his wallet, but instead of pulling out money, he showed me a badge. He then stood up and knocked on the door to the adjoining room.

Another man entered the room, and the first said, "You are under arrest." I was not handcuffed, but I was escorted downstairs to a waiting police car. I was booked, fingerprinted, and placed in a cell until the agency attorney came to release me.

I was quite upset by the whole ordeal because I hadn't done anything other than acknowledge I was sent by the agency and what the fee was. Sex was neither discussed nor an activity that took place. I just spoke a sentence or two, and now I had an arrest on my file.

It took a bit of lawyering, but the charges were dropped, my file was expunged, and I ended my – excuse the puns – brief, undercover under covers career. Everyone at the agency understood why I had to leave. I couldn't risk losing my military career, and this ordeal made it impossible for me to ignore the mounting risks.

As a thank you for our year of excellent service, DeWayne and I were taken on a four-day cruise with all expenses paid by the owner and her husband. The four of us ate, drank, and danced as we talked about the experiences of the last year.

All in all, I would say I never acted inappropriately. I'm glad that this agency and I were there to provide the companionship that other humans desired but couldn't find on their own. I filled a need, I was in charge of my body, and I was able to provide for my family and my community. I never regretted giving up those three-inch heels, though!

11

LITA: RETURN TO THE ARMY

RETURNING TO THE ARMY REQUIRED new uniforms, stricter physical standards, and enduring an emotional overload that I hadn't felt since basic training. I went right back to being a worthless lump of clay for the Training, Advising, and Counseling (TAC) officers and drill sergeants to mold or kick.

The attrition rate was high. I believe my class started with forty-five eager candidates, but only fifteen made the final cut eighteen months later. Our training was supposed to help us lead troops. I found the TAC officers to be too full of themselves, and I was grateful for the presence of the Drill Sergeants.

The TACs were Reserve Officers' Training Corps (ROTC) officers who had never spent any time enlisted. How anyone can lead without knowing how to follow is beyond me, so I am saddened to hear that all OCS training is now performed by ROTC officers.

One of my drill sergeants was a Vietnam vet, a tightly muscled man but of much shorter stature than Sergeant Dugger. Sergeant Dugger loomed over you and boomed in a commanding voice to keep your attention. Drill Sergeant F. merely gave a command from his crisply starched uniformed frame, complete with boots so shiny that you could use their reflection to shave or apply mascara.

From what I can recall, the majority of our time in OCS was devoted to Drill and Ceremony so we could direct troop movements. Although we knew by now how to 'fall in' or make facing movements like left face, right face, and about face, this time we needed to be able to give the orders to the troops that would be soon falling in under the guidon of our own platoons and companies. It took me some more time than others to recognize the difference between left and right as you were standing in front of a platoon.

This error in judgment caused more pain and suffering than I can explain. I'll ask you to put this book down for a few minutes, get down on your back, put your arms and legs up in the air and hold them there as long as you can. This was the 'dying cockroach position,' and it was one of TAC's favorites. Another was the obvious 'front leaning rest,' or push-up position. From this position, you could either actually perform as many push-ups as required, hold the position with your arms fully extended, or lower yourself to a plank position and hold it until your muscles convulsed in pain and you fell face first in the dusty road. One thing I never minded was this remedial training. I looked at it as character building. I actually paid more attention to how it affected the others suffering with me than the fatigue it brought to my various muscle groups. The Drill Sergeants always used the experience to actually teach a lesson. They never had us 'drop for 20' simply because there was extra time while waiting in formation.

One TAC officer, however, was a sadist who seemed to enjoy the torture sessions. He was particularly harsh on women. One afternoon, when I had the unsavory extra duty of shining the male staff latrine with my toothbrush, I found his crisply starched Battle Dress Uniform (BDU) hanging in the shower area. In the military, your names are sewn to the front of your shirts, so I knew it was his. Thinking of my opportunity for payback, I searched the latrine for anything that might be usable. The pipes were wrapped in asbestos tape to keep them from freezing. Asbestos is an irritant and I may or may not have taken some to rub along the inside of the BDU trousers along the inner thighs. Later after chow that TAC may or may not have been walking unsteadily as he tried to scratch an itch without losing his military bearing.

By regulation, a candidate could only miss one day of training in the eighteen-month course, and then only with prior authorization. For the roughly three-hour trip from our homes in northern Illinois to the course in Springfield, it made more sense to go as a group. This allowed us to save fuel, spend extra time going over assignments through verbal lightning round questioning games, and stay awake to arrive safely after a long training weekend. There were enough of us to warrant a bus, and being licensed to drive one, I drew a bus from the motor pool once a month for the trek.

One month we almost had a problem. On Thursday, the day before we were to drive down, I had to have emergency surgery for a kinked fallopian tube. It was a simple enough procedure, but I overestimated my ability to recuperate. I have always been in decent physical condition, and worked out with weights quite a bit in my twenties and thirties. Halfway to Springfield, though, I had horrible postsurgical pain and asked for the assistant driver to take over for me. I spent the last hour writhing in pain on the floor of the bus and tried to pass myself off as human once we arrived. I knew I couldn't afford to miss a day, as having two children, I felt it was best to keep the emergency day open in case one of them needed me. I sucked up the pain, took some over-the-counter medication, and got through the evening training. The next morning, however, when it was time to fall out for our mandatory run, I knew I was in trouble. Luckily for me, one of the TACs took pity on me, and assigned me to work in the office during the run. I must have looked like I needed the break, and I am forever grateful for his act of kindness. Maybe I pushed myself too hard at times, or worked through pain when I should have taken it easy. I was never easy on myself.

The high point of OCS for me was having more common sense and awareness than my fellow candidates during a field exercise. The low point of OCS was working with the administration in Springfield to make adjustments so that my commission date would fall within the required deadline for my age.

More than halfway through the eighteen-month training, we were assigned an extended field experience of land nav, or land navigation. This particular exercise had several twists compared to previous experiences. Like other land navs, this was tested. We had to conduct the exercise to standards that were set out for us in exact measured steps.

Typically, the land nav is a solo exercise, so getting caught collaborating with others for hints would disqualify you from earning a passing grade, otherwise known as a "no-go." You also always knew when land nav would be the next activity.

This day was filled from start to finish with excitement, anticipation, and dread.

We began the morning with PT and chow. We were then loaded into the rear of a deuce and a half. As we sat in two rows along the length of the truck bed, conversation quickly escalated as everyone wondered where we might be traveling.

The canvas was lifted on the rear of the deuce, the tailgate dropped, and in the grass at the rear of the truck stood our drill sergeants and two or three other NCOs with a presence that let you know they were combat-seasoned. Simultaneously, they all yelled at us, "Off the truck! Move! Over there! On the ground! Hands on your heads! Sit on the ground! Move! Move! Move!"

No one questioned them or hesitated. We all just did as we were told. Once we were all sitting on the ground, we were told to take off our boots, tie them together, and hand them over our heads to the NCOs circling behind us like vultures. The truck then departed, leaving the NCOs and us. Our boots taken, we were told to lie flat on the ground, heads down.

Looking up or around was not an option. We all got into the position we were instructed to take, and lay there awaiting further instructions.

I'm not sure how long we waited or who was the first to dare look up, but the eerie quiet after the raucous period before must have been the thing that triggered the curiosity.

"They're gone!" someone said, and we all stirred cautiously to an upright position. Off to the side rose a pile of our boots, a pile of Meals Ready to Eat, or MREs, a pile of full canteens, and enough envelopes so that a team of three could share.

Most went for the pile of boots. Our names were inside each in black permanent marker. I walked over to the envelopes. Inside, I found a topographical map, a compass, and instructions. We were to form teams of three. We were to follow the coordinates on the paper in the envelope, using the map and compass, and make our way to a base camp.

I took the contents of the envelope, grabbed an MRE and stowed it in the side leg pocket of my BDU pants, hooked a canteen to my web belt, and went to find my boots. The pile was smaller now, without as much frustration and cursing over whose boots were whose.

As I laced up my boots, I noticed that many were already teaming up and setting their coordinates. The two fellow classmates I teamed up with seemed very eager to move out. "This is probably timed," they agreed. They wanted to get to wherever we were heading right away!

There were some rules on the coordinates paper as well. You could not split up. If you did, you would be disqualified, and would have to undergo some type of remedial training. Your team would be scored by how many waypoints were correctly checked off. If you were caught using a hard road or street, points would be deducted from your score.

This sounded fair enough. We were off. We had to take turns on waypoints and initial off the ones we found. The first three were fairly easy. We were feeling confident, so we stopped to eat lunch. I ate the main part of my MRE, pocketing the snack, which was peanut butter spread in a pouch, and carb, which was hard crackers.

With food and water in us, we drew straws to see who would start us out again. I don't know who took that first turn, other than that it wasn't me, and we started out for the second half of the exercise. Since we were "following" the classmate with the map and coordinates, we had no way of knowing if anything was amiss. Based on how long this leg of the trek had taken, however, we began to have concerns when the shadows started lengthening off the trees.

We called ahead to our guide and asked if everything was OK, if we could help. He only replied that this was his point and that everything was fine. We allowed him a half hour more latitude but then called a halt to the progress and pulled together as a group to view the map and the coordinates he was following. After a fairly quick assessment, we realized we were in deep trouble.

My fellow observer and the last leader just about came to blows. Frustration ran high. I tried studying the map we were given and tried my hardest to figure out where we might be. I came up empty, and after the other two in my group calmed down a bit, I asked what they thought the best course of action would be.

Darkness was descending rapidly upon us, and we had to come to an agreement. The one who had just had his turn with the map kept silent. The other soldier chose to have us hike to the top of a hill not far off our current location. Perhaps we could see something from a higher vantage point. We hiked up a rather steep incline of heavy brush. I couldn't really tell if we had summited the peak, but one of the others saw a clearing if we took a turn and headed back down. We headed down through the now very dark foliage to what we hoped would be the end of our saga.

Upon reaching the bottom of the hill, we were not as relieved as we had hoped. It was in fact a clearing, but we saw no truck, no other troops, and nothing welcoming. We could see that this clearing was probably a mile or so in circumference, not completely circular, but it was surrounded on all sides by more trees and brush, more darkness. And now that we were out from under the tree canopy, we saw that it was clouding up. A hidden moon gave little illumination to the emptiness ahead.

"It's going to rain," said one. "We've got to get moving." And with that, he started a slow run into the field ahead.

"Wait!" I yelled, and the two who were now running in tandem ahead of me only turned their heads in acknowledgment but continued moving forward. "Stop!" I yelled with more insistence than I thought could come from my throat. They stopped dead in their tracks. They waited while I approached their position. I said quickly, "Something is wrong. Something is off. Can't you hear it?"

They looked at each other and then at me. "Hear what?"

I then yelled again, this time a simple, "Hello?" not expecting an answer. They were listening now, and they heard it too. If it were just a clearing ahead, it would have a different sound. Whatever lay ahead actually absorbed my sound. A lake?

We walked forward with more care, our boots landing first on grass and weeds but then on rock and gravel. I yelled again. Whatever it was, we were closer now. One of the other two picked up a large rock and tossed it. We all waited for the splash. No splash, but we heard it bounce off a wall of rock, chipping away pieces as it fell. He threw another. The same. We had stumbled upon a quarry. If my comrades had continued their jog, they might have experienced a serious injury, or worse!

We did an about face, retraced our steps to the tree line, and followed it around to get to the other side safely. As we approached the opposite side, we found a gravel road that was obviously leading in and out of the quarry. The two men did not want to get disqualified at this point, so we walked just inside the tree line but followed the contour of the road.

I was tired of the branches in my face and the unsure footing. Remedial training sounded wonderful to me right now! I had no idea of the time, but it was either very late or very early.

Shortly afterward, the sun started filtering through the trees. It was predawn, and I had a feeling that we were going to be catching hell for this escapade!

The gravel road emptied onto a rural road. It didn't look like much traffic ever passed by here. I guessed that meant we were still in the training area. I looked back and forth, up and down the road. With no real clues, I chose to go to the right.

The two men finally gave up the rules of the game, and the three of us walked easily down the middle of the street. A mile or so down the road, we came across a very welcome sight. There on our left was an obvious National Guard field kitchen, and the sounds and smells refreshed my once crushed spirit. As we turned and walked up to the men standing at the coffee pot filling cardboard cups with hot liquid, one of them spotted us and let out a yelp. They were actually happy to see us!

One was a full bird colonel, the other a sergeant major I had seen around Camp Lincoln.

"Are you OK, Mac?" asked the colonel.

"Yes, sir! Just hungry, sir," I replied. From what I can recall, there was no reprimand, just relief. I was handed a mess kit loaded with potatoes and eggs, which I took and then made my way to a tree across the muddy dirt road from the mess truck. As soon as I got to the middle of the road, my boot hit the edge of a water-filled tire rut. Down I slid into the rut until I was all but submerged in the muck.

My outstretched hand above that slimy water held my mess kit, still full of food. Someone took a picture of my dilemma, which I saw at some point during my final days at OCS. I would love to see that picture again someday.

Besides being an old recruit at Basic Combat Training back in 1977, it turned out that I was the oldest OCS trainee in my class. I kept up with the requirements and was near the top of my class throughout the program, but for me, this class was all or nothing. I was nearing the age limit for a soldier to be commissioned as an officer. I was so close, in fact, that if the commissioning ceremony was put off by two weeks, as was discussed due to the availability of its hall, I would have done this eighteen months for nothing. I petitioned the cadre to reconsider their proposed adjustment to the ceremony, and went into the final month with relief rather than dread.

The remainder of OCS was uneventful and rather pleasant. To celebrate the upcoming graduation, commissioning, and departure from Camp Lincoln, we went to a local barn/bar/dance establishment.

With blue jeans and gym shoes, we learned line dancing with the locals from a southern farm town of Illinois. There was a lot of beer, a lot of raw emotions, and there may or may not have been a naked hot tub party afterward with my TACs, drill sergeants, and me. Ahhhh, the good ol' memories of training!

We closed out the class and moved on to our next assignments as new 2nd Lieutenants in the Illinois Army National Guard. A 2nd Lieutenant typically has the responsibility of a platoon of soldiers to lead. In order to gain practical knowledge of the skillsets our soldiers had to work with day in and day out, we were told we required more training.

I now found myself in a similar situation to when I first joined in 1977: the needs of the military didn't coincide with my desires.

I wanted to stay in maintenance, since by now I had an associate's degree in diesel mechanics. The Illinois Army National Guard, however, needed new officers in communications.

After first being automatically assigned to the 133rd Signal Battalion, I had to submit a transfer request to a maintenance unit. The transfer took about six to nine months. During that time, I felt like a fish out of water, working with troops and equipment that reminded me of the radio my ex-husband used to toy with.

My company commander surprised and impressed me. He was only a First Lieutenant! We first met at a pre-drill weeknight meeting at the armory in Chicago. I dressed in my starched BDUs and highly polished boots to try and make an impression on the new commander. I entered the meeting room, and found a dozen or so individuals dressed in a variety of clothing, mostly casual, as if they were attending a concert or something. The room was full of smoke, as there were at least four members puffing on cigarettes. My commander introduced himself as soon as I entered. Lieutenant Tomas had on a casual button-down shirt of some pattern and grey pinstriped pants. *Who dresses this guy? He's the commander?* These were my only thoughts at the time. I took a seat at the far end of the long conference table and pulled out a notepad to take notes. Following that first meeting, everyone filed out and crossed the street to a local bar, where I joined them for beers. The stark contrast between OCS and this cluster of disorganized men and women made me feel that I had made a huge mistake. My orders still folded in my trouser pocket of my BDUs, I wondered how quickly I could transfer.

I didn't actually submit my transfer for a few months, as per advice, I was willing to give it a chance. The transfer was something I truly needed, however, if I was going to survive in the Guard. This particular unit was lacking in discipline and the Battalion Staff had no respect for my Company Commander. Each meeting and training weekend was the same. He was not just ignored, he was ridiculed! My heart went out to him. He was just a lieutenant! I did what I could to help for the short time I was there, and he was appreciative. After meetings, when we retreated to the bar across the street, I would sit near him and we would talk while the rest of the unit tuned us out.

The transfer wasn't going as well as I had hoped, as it turns out the Illinois Army National Guard was riddled with cronyism, and if you weren't in with the 'right group,' you didn't have as smooth of a ride. After six months or so of trying, I decided I couldn't take it any longer and 'jumped ship' from the Guard to the Army Reserves. My assignment was a maintenance unit in Joliet, about an hour's drive from my home.

I can't say much about this unit, as it turns out that this was merely a stepping stone in my career, one that got me registered for my Ordnance Officer Basic Course (OBC) in Aberdeen Proving Grounds Maryland. I never even met my platoon members; I just shipped directly to the course to become proficient in leading troops as mechanics in the Army.

In the Army, ordnance is the nomenclature for both artillery/armament and maintenance. I was taking the maintenance branch of Ordnance OBC. Upon completion of the course, I returned to Joliet for their final drill meeting as they were being disbanded and reassigned to units elsewhere. It was here I realized that as a Reservist, your assignment can be anywhere in the country, and there weren't many Army Reserve Units in the state. Rather than move out of state, I again transferred to the Illinois Army National Guard. This time, however, I was 'trained' after completing OBC, and given a position in the 108th Support Battalion in North Riverside, very near my home.

I served as a member of Battalion Staff as a Maintenance Officer. I now had the opportunity to help manage all maintenance requirements for Company B, 108th SPT BN, as well as the equipment used by the transportation unit and medical unit assigned to the 108th.

The first annual training assignment with my new unit took a hard turn just as we were getting ready to load our equipment for the trip to Fort McCoy. A deuce and a half driven by a soldier from the 133rd Signal Battalion was on its way back to Chicago from a rifle training mission in Marseilles when one of its front tires blew out. This caused the truck to overturn several miles from North Riverside. Being the closest unit, we were sent to retrieve the damaged truck. The soldier, thrown from the truck and killed instantly, was a member of my old unit. I didn't know him well, but it was still very hard to realize that a soldier had been lost, and all I could do was remove the bent metal that once carried him from his last duty station to his death.

I have seen people killed before in highway accidents. On a trip home from Fort Riley with my girls sleeping in the back seat of my 1965 Ford Galaxie 500, I was witness to a pedestrian vs car accident on the highway. The poor man was helplessly propelled probably 100 feet from the front grill of one car into the path of another in the opposite direction. Another time I was first on the scene of a horrific accident just after I left Fort McCoy, where two civilians were decapitated by a semi-truck that lost control, went airborne and sliced the top of their car off.

This time, however, it was one of "us," a fellow soldier, trying to get home to his family after spending two weeks in the heat of the Wisconsin forests. This was even more hard.

The newly promoted Captain Tomas, my old commander, came to North Riverside, where we had taken the truck following the accident. I could see the pain in his blue eyes as he assessed the damages. He was in his Class A uniform, and was on his way to notify the deceased next of kin.

After speaking to him briefly, I offered to drive him to the soldier's home. The ride was quiet, and not a word was spoken between us, as I could tell he was mentally preparing for this grim task ahead of him. I sat in the military blazer, known by us as a commercial utility cargo vehicle or CUCV, as he walked somberly to the doorway of the soldier's home.

When he returned, I could see tears welling in his eyes, and I reached over to grasp his hand, which was shaking. The return drive to the armory was just as quiet, but I felt good about my decision to drive him, since he was not in any condition to drive alone, or even to be alone. I asked if he wanted to go for a beer after we turned the CUCV into the motor pool. He agreed, and we went across the street to a local bar that this unit frequented after meetings. That day, I became friends with Captain Anton Tomas.

The blown-out tire turned out to be the first of several that would cause accidents throughout the state in the weeks leading up to Annual Training (AT). A State Maintenance Officer was assigned to determine what was causing the damage and trauma. He soon discovered that most of the tires in the fleet of trucks and trailers in the state had retread tires on their axles, and the top layer of rubber was separating as the vehicles moved down the road, causing the tires to fail. My new task for the entire summer was to work side by side with the State Maintenance Officer to inventory and arrange for replacement of any tires found to be within the date range and brand of the previous tires that failed.

I sent out a Memorandum of Record to each of the company commanders in the 108th, directing them to inventory each tire and turn in the list prior to departing for AT. Any tires found to be faulty would need to be swapped out with new tires that the state acquired and had delivered to each of the maintenance units.

Upon reaching Fort McCoy, however, I discovered some inconsistencies in reporting by one of the commanders in my Battalion. It turned out this unit actually still had trucks operating that had not yet been retrofitted with new rubber! I went to the commander with a copy of the Memorandum I had sent out a month earlier, and asked if he was aware of the seriousness of the problem. His response was, "I don't take orders from a staff puke, especially a female! You are as useless as tits on a bull. Now, get out of my TOC!"

The Tactical Operations Center, or TOC, was the remote office set up in a GP Large tent each commander used to control his or her unit's activity. I was furious, but being outranked, I retreated to Battalion Headquarters and reported my findings (and the response) to my superior, the Battalion Commander. I was relieved to see I had his support, and not only did the unit immediately begin to comply with the directives, but also, the commander was forced to make a formal apology in formation so that everyone who overheard the harmful remarks knew that that type of discrimination was not tolerated in this Battalion.

I was doing a great deal of driving from unit to unit throughout the training area to check the status of the tire swaps. One afternoon, as I was driving through the garrison area, I slowed as I approached a soldier on a raggedy bicycle with wide tires and faded paint. By the color of the bike, I assumed it was from the MWR (Morale, Welfare, & Recreation) section of McCoy. As I slowly passed the cyclist, my eyes caught sight of the rank on his cap. *A MAJOR?!* I thought, *what was a Major doing on a piece of crap bike when I was a lowly Lieutenant in a CUCV?*

I pulled to the curb ahead of the man and hopped out of the driver's seat, rushing over to render a salute. "Sir, can I give you a ride?" I asked. He returned my salute and I stood even more dumbfounded than I was a minute ago. Now his name tape caught my attention. "Pritzker" was evident in black letters across his right breast pocket. A Chicago native, I was very familiar with the name of the philanthropist family. It was emblazoned on the walls of museums, hospitals, and schools, and here this Major was riding a broken MWR bike at Fort McCoy!

He smiled and said hello, and asked how my AT was going. I explained my duties, to which he replied something to the effect of

"Ahhhh, Logistics! So easily overlooked, but critically important!"

After that, he spoke at some length about the requirements for running a mess hall or a restaurant, and how even minute details could lead to disaster if not given appropriate attention.

"Attention to detail," I replied in agreement. Then I repeated my question, asking if he needed a lift.

He waved away the offer by explaining he actually loved riding. It was his favorite form of PT. He thanked me for the offer, and bid adieu as he hopped back on the torn saddle of the bike.

I would always have positive memories of the day and situation that brought me to first meet Major J. Pritzker. Conversation came very easily, and I was very impressed by his commitment to service and self.

During this annual training, I built a closer relationship with Anton. Although we weren't in the same unit any longer, we had stayed in touch through casual phone calls. He and I would drive around the compound at night, patrolling to ensure soldiers were not acting unruly and being the Officers-on-call for emergencies for our units.

One night we parked at the end of the block of barracks, and I reached over and gave him a kiss. He returned the kiss warmly, and with some hesitation, reached inside my BDU top. He was very hesitant in his actions, and I felt the need to offer constant reassurance.

We didn't do anything else for the remaining time at camp, but he called to ask me out for dinner once we got back home.

The dating was strained. I felt like I was making all of the physical advances, and he was taking my lead. I hadn't experienced such a laissez-faire attitude in relationships with men, except when I was working with men on the autism spectrum years before!

I asked questions during the first few dates, and discovered I was in fact the second woman he had been with. The first was many years prior, and a one-night stand. I allowed myself to be drawn in by his complete naïveté. Dinners turned into longer dates at my home, where we would sit for hours talking. He had a strong moral compass, however, and we never did more than kissing, with some occasional full body caresses. It felt good to be in the company of someone who appeared to respect women and cared about what I had to offer the world as a mother, an officer, and a friend.

12

LITA: COMPANY COMMAND

IF AN OFFICER REMEMBERS ONLY one thing about their military experience, it is their first command. That is what I had trained for! Being a company commander in the Illinois Army National Guard is very different from serving in an active-duty position. For one thing, the soldiers who are assigned to your unit are part-timers with full-time lives outside of the Army.

Following my year as a maintenance officer for the 108th, I returned to training, and took the Officer Advanced Course, Company Commander Course, and Junior Maintenance Officer Courses.

As a fully vetted and trained ordinance officer, I was assigned to a maintenance company: Bravo Company of the 108th Support Battalion, Illinois Army National Guard. I had 159 soldiers, an assortment of vehicles, an office, a supply room, a weapons armory, and a mission requirement to maintain the equipment of the battalion.

For the non-mechanics reading this, know that for a mechanic, having a toolbox fills you with enormous pride. A nice setup gives you an air of professionalism. People see your toolbox, and they know that you take pride in what you do.

Equally important is how well the toolbox and tools are maintained. After finishing service every day, service techs clean and organize their tools. Doing so makes for less work the next day and faster access to the tools they'll need, and in wartime, efficiency is of the utmost importance. So during my first week as a company commander, imagine my shock to find there were bare-bones, limited tools!

Luckily, the month before, I had taken a course called Company Command, and in that course, one theme stood out like no other. When you take command, if you don't have the time to conduct a proper inventory, you are able to request a three-person team from Springfield to assist.

My first official order to my supply sergeant: "Request a support team from Springfield!" The team wouldn't arrive until the next week. My MTOE property book was still unsigned. If I signed it, I owned it!

The rule of thumb for a company commander was to expect to pay one-month active duty pay when they rotated out of command for lost equipment during their tenure. Many years afterwards, looking at a *Reserve Component Equipment Shortages* report of 2016, the Army National Guard as a whole was 22.5% short of their required equipment.

At the time, I knew I wasn't alone in the dilemma of being underequipped, but that knowledge didn't matter for two reasons: firstly, I am a mechanic. I was one in the active Army, and I know how it feels to have the right tools for the job, and secondly, I was going to do things by the book.

My battalion's property book officer was young, a newly commissioned 2nd Lieutenant if I remember correctly. He took his job a bit too seriously. He called and complained on a daily basis for me to sign for the company, meaning that I needed to sign hand receipts accounting for everything the maintenance company had been issued.

We all know what rolls downhill, and I guess the State Property Office was after him, so he had to be after me to get it done. I waited, and felt relief when the state inspection team arrived. As an incoming commander, an officer receives three days of active duty pay to complete the turnover process. I had already put in over a week with no pay just to get an idea of what I needed to do as a new boss to 159 mechanics.

I now took my three days of paid time and went through the supply department shelf by shelf, item by item, truck by truck, toolbox by toolbox. At the end of those three days, the team wrote up a report stating that approximately $459,000 worth of personal hand tools and testing equipment appeared to be missing.

They had to say approximately, because most of the inventory checklists were also missing. There was no legitimate way to know what was missing as far as tools were concerned. I thanked them and signed for my company.

My next task as a commander was to set up training. A Guard soldier only trains two days a month and two weeks in the summer. The training is job related. In other words, how would our unit perform in case of war or other national emergency?

Most of the training is at the lower levels—individual, squad, and platoon—but sometimes, training with other units provides a more integrated training scenario. I could request outside forces, either active or reserve, to test the unit for levels of competency. These test not only the individual soldiers, but also the unit as a whole. The goal, again, is to discover how the unit would act in case of mobilization.

Once a disaster or war is declared, National Guard troops are mobilized to full-time status and are integrated into other units to create a force that can accomplish whatever the larger mission happens to be. Luckily, my first sergeant was an expert infantryman, a Green Beret, a Vietnam veteran, and a full-time mechanic at a local car dealership. In other words, on the training side, I had the best of the best by my side!

Sergeant First Class Raymond Maurer was my right hand, and the company respected him. I felt it was my responsibility to arm the troops with the tools they needed to succeed. That feeling would drive me to do my very best in this new leadership position.

One thing in my favor was an extensive amount of free time to devote to my unit. I had recently married Anton (Tony) Tomas, who was then a Major and with the 85th Training Division of the Army Reserves in Arlington Heights, Illinois.

We married, February 17, 1990 in a Presbyterian Church to which he belonged. It was a decently sized wedding, since my family attended. My family now numbered near 250, with aunts, uncles, and cousins included. On his side were his mother, his aunt and a cousin. I believe shell-shock is the right term for when his family finally met mine. Outnumbered eighty to one and louder than a five-piece brass band, my family dominated the reception. Although he may have felt overwhelmed, this wedding had the family stamp of approval and Tony was welcomed by everyone in attendance. This was a much better second round.

Tony worked full time for U.S. Customs as an export inspector since 1977. He had good seniority and a good income to match. With my husband providing for our basic needs, I took a leave from my full-time mechanic's job. I devoted full-time hours in the North Riverside Armory which housed my unit's company office, supply room, and maintenance shop.

There, I forged stronger than usual friendships with all of the full-time staff from the battalion level down, as well as with the full-time mechanics who worked in the regional maintenance shop adjacent to our office building and drill floor.

One day, while stopping by the maintenance shop, I picked up a current copy of PS Magazine. The PS, or Preventative

Maintenance Monthly, was a comic book formatted for mechanics and logistics personnel. There would be tips on repairs, and maintenance suggestions. The issue I paged through had an advertisement of sorts, and the headline got my attention: "Free Tools!" It was from the Rock Island Arsenal. They were giving out surplus tools recovered from the first Gulf War to units if they showed the need.

I could hardly believe my eyes! We were only a few weeks away from AT and my troops might have tools in their toolboxes? I called the number in the advertisement, found out where to fax my request, and set off gathering a list of 'must-haves,' from socket sets to multimeters.

I sent my training NCO with an empty semi-trailer to the arsenal just days before we were leaving for Fort McCoy. Upon arrival at our training site, I had the semi doors open and had the personnel bring their empty tool boxes to be replenished. I told them all to personally keep track of what they were given since using hand receipts in the field would have been both time consuming and difficult in the driving rain. Thinking as a mechanic, I knew they would just be glad to have tools to use for a change and didn't worry about entrusting them with the new tools til we could properly inventory back at our home base in a few weeks. I felt like Santa giving toys to kids. It was a great relief to me and my NCOs knowing we could actually get some work done!

However, the feeling deflated quickly several days later when the State Property Book Officer, we will just call him "Lemon," found out and came raging into my tent.

This young, overzealous Officer was also the one that was in charge of my unit's equipment and was of no help whatsoever at the time of my taking over command. If I had considered him an ally perhaps I would have considered approaching his office for assistance, but my short history with him showed that he was a figurehead and nothing more. I am a person that gets things done and when I saw an opportunity to fill the gaps in my inventory, I took it.

Lemon wanted to know what and who gave me the authority to do what I had just done. I pulled out the PS Mag from my hip pocket and showed him. He explained that what I did should have come from him. It seemed that he took offense to my being in command, out ranking him, and perhaps to my even being a woman.

I said, "Well, you didn't see it, or didn't take the initiative so . . ." Yeah, that went over like a lead balloon. I tried in vain to refute his claims of who was wrong and who was right in this case. Ultimately, I had to take back all the tools I had passed out a few days prior.

I was crushed. I felt abused by a system of red-tape and bureaucracy that was now stopping my mechanics from work. I don't have a clue where those tools ended up, but our inventory and so ability remained limited throughout my time in command.

Despite challenges like these, being in tune with the mission statements, movement orders, and requirements for my segment of the larger battalion as soon as they were received from brigade headquarters gave my unit an edge over the other units.

I also had an opportunity to work on building strength in our company roster. As commander, I was required to keep my personnel staffed at a given level and oversee recruitment and retention. I discovered that most of my troops came from the inner city of Chicago, although the unit trained in the near west suburbs.

Often, individual soldiers experienced transportation problems getting to and from the unit. I assisted in calling on troops that had poor attendance, worked with them on a one-on-one basis, and assisted in any way I could to ensure they met their requirements for the contracts they had signed. I got to know my soldiers and their families, and I passed on any pertinent information to my first sergeant.

Sergeant First Class Ray Maurer, may he rest in peace, was a keen judge of character. Soft-spoken, but with an air of authority from seeing combat in the jungles of Nam, he won our unit's respect. We made a good command structure for the company to follow. Other personnel who helped me achieve a successful command included soldiers assigned full-time to the unit: Sergeants Kimberly Broome, Jean Grant, and DeWayne Walton.

Without these three handling the training, supply, and admin portions of the company, we could have easily failed. It takes a solid connection between the full-time active-duty soldiers and the M-Day or weekend warriors, as the rest of us Guardsmen were called. Without us all pulling together, work could not be completed.

Along with these three steadfast soldiers, I had an entire full-time maintenance shop, manned by more active-duty soldiers, working on our equipment during the nine-to-five Monday through Friday workweek. My advice to all reserve or Guard soldiers: take care of your full-timers, and they will take care of you!

13
LITA: WHEN IT COUNTS

I HATED TO LEAVE MY command, but it is considered a stepping stone in one's career. After my time there was up, it was time to move on to the next step. I had experienced such a good tour as company commander and wanted it to continue forever. It always instilled a sense of pride in my troops when I would march in front of the company as we would prepare for a company run. My guidon, the flag with the crimson red B embroidered under the numbers 108, would be retired. The new company in the newly designated Battalion would be the 3625th Maintenance Company.

Just before it became time to turn over the guidon to the next commander, another rite of passage loomed. Officers and noncommissioned officers get performance reviews as in any major corporation. Officers work exceptionally hard to attain top marks in all portions of the review. Three officers having even higher rank and responsibility than the rated officer sign off and grade the Officer Evaluation Report, or OER.

In my case, my battalion commander served as my rater, my brigade commander served as my intermediate rater, and the adjutant general for the State of Illinois performed the role of my senior rater.

The procedure should have gone according to the book, but I found out that my battalion commander, the man who had harassed me before, had his own way of working. The other two company commanders received stellar reports, but mine was subpar. When I asked why I didn't get what I thought I deserved, I was told simply, "You can improve it if you sleep with me."

I had not felt so violated since I joined the service and didn't know what to do, if anything.

I reported the incident to the full-time admin officer, who in turn brought it to the attention of whoever needed to know further up the chain of command.

My husband also showed up at the North Riverside Armory one day after work. He was there to inform my battalion commander that I would in fact not be sleeping with him to improve my OER. Although he and my commander were of equal rank in the military, my battalion commander was in this instance quite literally outgunned. It seems that in coming right from work, my husband had forgotten that he was still in his U.S. Customs uniform, complete with badge, handcuffs, and pistol. He told my commander exactly what he thought about sexual harassment.

After being corrected from both inside the chain of command and from my husband, my OER was adjusted to correctly review my abilities.

The battalion commander was transferred out of the unit, and sadly, he was promoted and given a higher command position in Springfield. I wondered how a person with such character could continue to rise through the ranks and be given even more responsibility. I also wondered if the Illinois Army National Guard was still the right fit for me as I considered my future.

There was one final task before I rotated out of the command slot: the change of command inventory. When I went through

OBC, they made one thing crystal clear: before you take command of a unit, you have to have an accurate inventory of all assigned equipment and property. That includes every vehicle, tool, blanket, and bullet on the inventory list or hand receipt. If you don't put eyes on each and every item, and simply assume that everything's there, you could be held financially accountable, and have to pay out of pocket for anything that might have gone missing over the years. If the total value of missing equipment is great enough, it can result in time in jail. That lesson really stuck with me, and I requested a special team from the state to assist with my incoming inventory. If it wasn't for the diligent team that assisted me, and all of their hard work, this story would have a different ending. I might be writing this from a cell at Fort Leavenworth, but that assistance visit and the report of missing inventory they left with me were my saving grace!

Instead of having to take responsibility for the Report of Survey, which was essentially a bill for any equipment lost under my command, in this case for almost a half a million dollars, I rotated out virtually unscathed. The initial Report of Survey shocked me, since everyone up and down the chain of command knew the story behind the lack of equipment. But there again was the State Property Book Officer, Lemon, trying to ruin my life.

I took my concern, and the unjust $500,000 bill, to the adjutant general in his Springfield office. He asked me to go for a walk with him as we discussed. He suggested we take the stairs in the "Puzzle Palace," which is what the M-Day soldiers called the concrete maze of offices. Once in the concrete stairwell, he stopped and turned to me.

"Lita, my hands are tied. There is nothing I can do. I would if I could."

Shocked even more than I was on the drive to Springfield, I drove home and considered my options. I never really understood why he couldn't correct this injustice, but if I dwelled on that, I wouldn't be solving my problem.

My immediate thought was that I needed an attorney. I decided to go outside of the National Guard system in case the issue was too large or too close for objectiveness within its confines. I went to an Army Reserve unit in a nearby town and talked to a JAG (judge advocate general) officer stationed there.

The JAG officer gave me advice, wrote a letter that agreed with my initial statement that this equipment has been missing for many, *many* years, made copies of everything, and forwarded it to the board that would be meeting to discuss my case.

In the end, I won my case.

I would never know what happened with the shortage. It was probably written off. The experience, however, convinced me that it was time to abandon ship! I realized once again that the cronyism still existed, and I just didn't fit in.

I did not stay in the Illinois Army National Guard. I instead took a position in an Army Reserve unit. To make the change I also needed to take on a position I didn't consider myself qualified for; but just to get out from under the bureaucracy was worth whatever effort I had to make. I joined the Fighting Eighty-fifth, Custer Division!

The Eighty-fifth Training Division in Arlington Heights, Illinois, was very heavy in office work and had little to no maintenance activity, convoys, or typical formations to start and end the day. We showed up to work as if it were a corporation headquarters. The chain of command existed, I am sure, but it was not an obvious part of the unit activity.

From 2000 to 2002, my task as the unit admin officer was to collect, process, store, display, and disseminate information that flowed continuously into the headquarters. Well, that might have been the function of the full-time officer. I ran the mail room on drill weekends. In a way I guess it was a well-deserved rest from the emotional trauma I had just left, but it was not challenging, and I needed a challenge.

I discovered that the division also had command of the military funeral honors for our part of the state. I quickly became trained in the procedures for the teams that visited the local funeral homes or cemeteries, then learned what it took to run the entire program.

The individual who had been performing this job was leaving, so I stepped up and volunteered to take it over. To do this, I was put on a year and a half of month-to-month orders, giving me a full-time job besides my weekend position in admin.

That said, in the military there is a rule: "NEVER volunteer." Volunteering was something that inevitably got you into trouble or into a position you wouldn't give to your worst enemy. But my experience might have been the one and only exception to that rule. I absolutely loved my position! I had freedom to run the assignment as I found fit for the circumstances. I conducted training and coordinated with our local veterans cemetery, Abraham Lincoln National Cemetery, near Joliet, Illinois.

I stood in for team members if they were out sick, and I learned of the important services provided by agencies like the American Legion, Veterans of Foreign Wars, and Disabled American Veterans. These volunteers augment at military funerals, and the respect they show as they assist is unparalleled.

While stationed at the Eighty-fifth, my daughter Jean Marie was finishing up her Chemical Officer Basic Course at Fort Leonard Wood, Missouri. She had already completed OCS in the Illinois Army National Guard, and as a newly commissioned officer she was learning the specific technical skills she would need to become a qualified chemical officer.

It was April 2000. Jean had just a few days to go. That month, I planned to drive down for her class completion ceremony, but before I could do that I received an unexpected phone call. It was the base hospital at Leonard Wood. Jean had been injured in some type of training accident.

Lita's step-father, John Scaro, ~1952

Lita's maternal uncle, Robert 'Butch' Wendell, 1959

Lita and her mother, Genevieve, 1957   *Lita, First Catholic Communion, 1961*

Lita getting ready for high school graduation, with her step grandparents,
John R. Scaro, Sr. and Jeanette Scaro, 1972

Lita pregnant with Jean, 1973

Jean Marie, Genevieve, Jeanette, Lita, and Kym, 1975

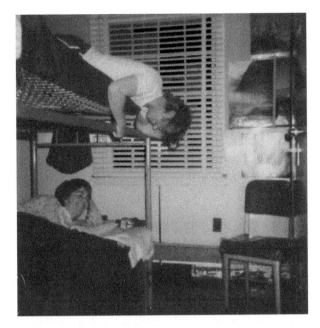

Lita and Ginny Lingle, Basic Training, Ft. Jackson, SC, 1977

Lita sitting on steps to women's barracks, Ft. Jackson, SC, 1977

Lita turning the tables and ordering Drill Sergeant, SFC Dugger, to do pushups, Ft. Jackson, SC, 1977

Lita and Wooten working on an M35 Deuce, Ft. Riley, KS, 1979

Lita and a favorite squad leader,
SSG Mullanax, Ft. Riley, KS, 1979

Jean, Lita, and Kym at the wedding
of Lita's sister, Linda, 1980

Jean, Oak Park, IL, 1982

Lita in Air Force uniform, Eglin
AFB, FL, 1984

Jean with pigeons, Greece, 1984

*Lita with bodyguard and driver
DeWayne Reynolds on a cruise, 1986*

Four of Lita's OCS TAC officers, Camp Lincoln, Springfield, IL, 1986

Lita's OCS platoon in front leaning rest, Ft. Jackson, SC, 1986

Lita, at OCS graduation, Camp Lincoln, Springfield, IL, 1986

Kym, Anton, Lita, and Jean, 1991

Jean, enlisted official photo, 1994

Jean hosting OCS graduation picnic,
Camp Lincoln, Springfield IL, 1999

*Devin, Dave, Kym, Jean, and Sean; Jean's OCS graduation,
Camp Lincoln, Springfield, IL, 1999*

Lita, Jean, and Anton, 2000

*Lita and Alex Moerle, high school algebra teacher turned
into lifelong friend, 2019*

JEAN

14
JEAN: IF THE BOOT FITS

IN MAY OF 1974, I was born at McGaw hospital, Loyola Medical Center, in Maywood, Illinois. My sister Kym was born the following fall. I have no memories of my parents as a married unit. As far back as I can remember, they were at one another's throats and in a heated custody battle. The only time I recall seeing them together was at court, alongside their attorneys.

When I was four and my sister was three, our mom was stationed in Kansas as a tank mechanic with the First Infantry Division, also known as the Big Red One. I remember early morning wake-ups, well before dawn, and time spent playing house with the wooden kitchen set at daycare. There, my sister and I were first exposed to a wide variety of ethnic, racial, and religious groups. At daycare, we played with children from around the globe. Our friends hailed from Korea, Singapore, all over Europe, Samoa, Guam, and Puerto Rico. For some of our classmates, English was a second language. We found, however, that play is a universal language.

Kym and I were often picked up by an officer, Nate Foster,

who was our mom's new friend. Nate was an Army reservist who trained out of Fort Riley and the owner of several rental properties in Junction City, Kansas. He even owned the property we lived in, so he was our landlord, too.

His hobby was powerlifting, and he had won numerous world championships. I can recall that his biceps were enormous. He could eat like a fiend and clear several entrees in one sitting! He would take turns carrying my sister and me over his head, as if we were barbells! He may have had little finesse when hauling human children around, but we did not mind.

Although I was only four years old at the time, I still have vivid memories of my mother standing in formation at the end of the day. Her entire platoon of mechanics lined up in tidy rows behind the huge garage they used to repair trucks and tanks. At exactly the same time each day, they would all become very quiet, their faces would appear more solemn, and in unison, they would salute the flag as taps played.

Nate, with ramrod posture, also saluted the flag. My sister and I would hold hands, stand quietly, and place a hand over our hearts until the final tones of taps reached our ears. We showed pride in our country at a very early age.

Weekends were more relaxed, but we still had military influence. All of the soldiers my mom worked with at the Fort during the week would come to our trailer and grill burgers, work on cars, and play horseshoes. But without fail, at four—or 1600, as they called it in military time—they would stop what they were doing, face the direction of the Fort, salute, and stand still for the time it would take to play taps.

I guess after doing it for so long, you just knew how long that would take. If we were on post shopping and it was time for retreat to play and the colors to be retired—when they brought the flag down for the night—shoppers would stand by their cars, face where the Fort headquarters was positioned, and render salutes.

Besides these daily formations and weekend barbecues, our time at Fort Riley, Kansas, was quiet and happy.

Unfortunately, our father did not care about our happiness. We were possessions and tools he used to cause our mother pain. He was also a monster from whom I would hide my sister when he was drunk. Our plastic turtle shaped toy box worked well as a hiding spot. I withstood the abuse to save my little sister from the same horrors I tolerated.

My biological father did not support my mother's decision to join the military. In the end, she was forced to give up her position in the Army. Our father had been making it harder and harder for her to keep us in Kansas. To appease him, we ended up moving back to the Chicago area.

We learned that in the courts, you often get what you pay for. I think the judge who presided over the majority of my parents' custody battle was later charged with taking bribes as part of Operation Greylord. Our father had money and the support of his family. Our mother was scraping by and had no one in her corner. She may have had right on her side, but Lady Justice is blind, and her scales can be manipulated. Our father wanted us to live near him, and in the end his attorney was more skilled than our mother's attorney. At one court hearing, my father's attorney even stopped and apologized to my sister and me.

Our departure from Fort Riley was rather sudden and trying, especially for our mother. That summer, I became very ill with scarlet fever, and lost my hearing. Although I made a full recovery, and my hearing eventually returned, I have lived with an auditory processing disorder since then. This makes it hard to understand what people are saying. To me, everything sounds like a jumble of sounds, and it takes time for me to process what is being said. I think reading and audiobooks have helped me greatly. Learning has always been a challenge and spelling has always been difficult.

During the fall of 1979, we were living in Bolingbrook, Illinois, and I soon started school. Kym attended preschool, and I was in kindergarten classes near our new home. Bolingbrook was an agricultural area at that time, and felt worlds away from Chicago. We watched the fields of corn grow a bit more each day on our way to school.

My mom found it difficult to make it on her own, working to support two children. We ended up moving to Oak Park, Illinois, with our maternal grandparents and their seven other children.

My aunts and uncles frequently took the time to remind my sister and me that we were not "really" family. Though they never explained that position, in reality they were our mother's half-brothers and sisters and therefore blood relatives. They all had the same mother. Instead of caring for family, they made us feel like we were a drain on their resources and not much more.

One of my uncles would try to get my sister and me to fist fight each other, and offered monetary rewards if we could land a good punch. When that didn't work, he would coach us to say utterly inappropriate or offensive phrases, and then send us off to repeat them to our grandmother. We would then endure various punishments like having our mouths washed out with soap or sent to bed early.

We moved in with our grandparents in 1980, and stayed there on and off for the next six years. They owned a five bedroom, one and a half bath bungalow which was built in 1914, on the Southside of Oak Park. With eleven of us typically living there at any one time, it was tight quarters.

We slept in the basement across from the laundry area. The basement laundry area and half bath were poorly lit, perpetually damp, gloomy, dank, and inhospitable. No one ever wanted to use the basement bathroom. So, as you can imagine, it was a challenge to accommodate eleven people who were all clamoring to use the bathroom in the morning.

With one window air conditioning unit in the living room/

dining room, the house was very hot in the summer. My sister and I would camp out under the table right next to the air conditioning unit on hot nights to try and stay cool. With so many children coming and going all day and night, the doors of the house were never locked. We had one television in the front room and two phones in the hall for entertainment. The small kitchen was a lovely avocado green, with banquette seating in the corner and a rollout dishwasher.

There was always a pot of coffee brewing, as my grandfather was in coffee sales, and by the time we could read we were dipping graham crackers in our cups o' joe. My aunts and uncles all worked in some capacity, and went to school. They were all older than me by five to fourteen years, but they seemed much older.

John, then twenty, was always smiling and by far our best babysitter. When he would watch us he always thought up games to play or adventures we could take. He is a very talented artist and was primarily away at college, or in Europe, fine tuning his talents.

Linda, nineteen, average height, average weight, has her late father's brown eyes and Italian mannerisms. She was dating, going to cosmetology school full time, and rarely home.

Frank, then eighteen, was the tallest of the group. He was focused on fitness, basketball, and always trying to come up with a way to make a quick buck. He had a huge boa constrictor, which often slithered out of its aquarium for the warmth of the kitchen refrigerator or the cool damp of the basement. Frank was a terrible babysitter.

Mike, then seventeen, has his mother's blond hair and his late father's metabolism. Mike was rarely home and his bedroom was a disaster zone. To get to his bed he had to wade through the piles of clothing and other detritus on the floor. He once lost a hamster in his room and paid me five dollars to try and find it. Mike had, at that time, what I thought of as the best job in the world. He was in high school and worked at the Lake Street movie theater.

At the end of his shift he got to bring home any leftover popcorn. *Free movies and popcorn, what could be better?*

Mary, then fifteen, was always tiny, petite, with long brown hair and soulful brown eyes. She's always been a fiend for cleaning. Her large collection of Madame Alexander dolls were in immaculate condition and housed in their own glass fronted cabinet. In my mind, Mary's always worked as a dental assistant, attired in a pristine white dental smock, with perfectly straight and bright white teeth.

Geniece, thirteen, stood out from her brothers and sisters with pale blond hair and big brown eyes. She's always had the positive outlook and the heart of a cheerleader. She was our grandmother's favorite, had the best clothes, and her own extensive collection of Madame Alexander dolls. Mary and Geniece were our resources for questions about boys, make-up, clothes, and puberty.

Bobby, the youngest of my grandparent's children at eleven in 1980, was a scrapper. He was smaller than all of his brothers and sisters, and always getting into fist fights to try and prove himself. I will always picture him in the boxing ring or coming home at night out of breath and dripping wet after he had sneaked into Rehm or Ridgeland pool after hours.

My mother didn't have a lot of choices when it came to finding someone to care for Kym and me. She had to spend long stretches of time on Active Duty for training and I think familial babysitters seemed like the safest option.

I never knew where I fit in in the family. My mom was paying my grandparents rent, yet I always felt like we were intruders and that we didn't belong. No one ever asked us how we felt when our mom was away. No one ever tried to console us or let us know that she'd be back soon. *Why not have a calendar and count down the days until her return? Why didn't anyone fix up the unfinished basement and make it more comfortable and less scary for two little girls? Why couldn't someone sit down and read to us? Why was it so hard to show us affection?*

It was utterly bizarre and alien to watch years later as my cousins were showered with a love and affection of which I thought my grandparents completely incapable. Where we were given dowdy clothes and made to feel guilty and beholden for any food we received, my cousins were given pretty clothes, trips to Disney World, and endless positive attention.

I'm sure my grandparents were feeling the strain of having two more mouths to feed and house. My uncles were probably tired of having to keep an eye on us, and our aunts probably didn't want us to damage their toys. But at the time, it felt like a cold place. I cried a lot and then was punished for crying.

One day, when I was seven years old, I was washing a mountain of dishes when I grabbed a sharp knife. I stood at the sink with my back to the room and considered taking my own life. *How hard could it be to slit my wrists?* I wondered. But, I talked myself out of it as I could not leave my sister alone.

During this period, the great outdoors was my escape. Every year my mom would take my sister and me camping. We hiked over sand dunes in Indiana, through forests in Wisconsin, Alabama, and Michigan, and across the network of bridges that connected the Florida Keys. In late spring, we would follow the deer trails that crisscrossed the forests in Wisconsin. Occasionally, we'd stop to search through the leaf mounds at the base of old aspen, elms, ash, and oak trees for delectable morel mushrooms.

In the winter, when we drove from the ice and cold of Chicago to the sun-soaked sands of the Florida Keys, my sister and I were in charge of navigation. Our mom would hand over the map book, and even though she knew the route by heart, she would allow us to supply the driving directions.

When I was nine or so years old, my sister Kym, our nanny, Ann, and Ann's son all headed to Greece with my mom. Mom had met Ann the previous year while she was working at an air base in Georgia. Ann hailed from Alabama and always had a smile, proper attire, oversized spectacles, and her auburn hair in a beehive updo. She loved the idea of taking a working vacation overseas with her son.

Our trip was thoroughly planned. My sister and I each had to write a report, and learned about the mythology, history, geography, architecture, cuisine, culture, language, and theater of Greece. Our mom was stationed on Crete with her engineering unit from the Air Force. She had traveled overseas via military transport, while our nanny and her son had flown commercial with my sister and me in tow.

Ann was a take-charge kind of person, and we felt very safe with her for that long flight. She kept track of us as we did the whole tourist thing, and we were able to spend time with our mom in the evenings.

We visited the ruins of old temples, admired the patchwork quilt of the terraced farms which blanketed the mountains, and spent countless hours visiting various museums. Still, there was enough time to swim in the hotel pool, which overlooked the Mediterranean Sea. I can still recall the small shrimp that swam in the pool, which was filled with seawater straight from the Mediterranean! On the weekends, my mother's unit would gather around the pool, laughing, telling stories, and thoroughly enjoying their time in Greece.

Unfortunately, our trip took an unexpected turn.

Mom developed a high fever and could not get out of bed. We were in our nanny's care and did not realize how serious the situation was at the time. We would later learn that she had appendicitis. She actually risked flying back home for surgery and is very, very lucky to have lived to tell the tale.

Not long after our return from the Greek Isles, my mom switched over from the Air Force Reserves to the Illinois Army National Guard.

This was about the time when she applied to be an officer and started Officer Candidate School in Springfield, Illinois. By the time I was twelve, she became a commissioned officer. We drove down to Springfield for the commissioning. She allowed my sister and me to pin on her gold bars during the ceremony. It was exciting to see my mom in her class A uniform with its shiny buttons and colorful ribbons. I was very proud of her.

Twelve years later, I would be back in Springfield working toward my own commissioning. But more about that later.

Although the saying "look before you leap" has been around since the 1500s, I have yet to heed its warning. I've always been a leap and damn the consequences type of gal!

In the summer of 1986, my grandparents, uncles and aunts, along with my sister and I drove the fifty-eight miles from Oak Park, Illinois to our small three-bedroom, one-bath cottage near Wonder Lake. Perched at the top of a hill, on Marblehead Road, the cottage was our summer escape from the Chicago heat. As I'd done in years past, as soon as we arrived, I wanted to jump in the lake. I changed into my swimsuit and grabbed a musty smelling beach towel from the hall closet. With glee, I ran down the steep hill to the beach. I held my breath as I ran past the spooky abandoned cabin near the bottom of the hill, which we believed to be haunted, and tried to reduce my speed as I slid on the loose gravel road.

At the private park-cum-beach, a thirty-foot tall mulberry tree stood sentinel over sunbathers, swimmers, and occasional fishermen. I negligently tossed my towel on the grass, slipped out of my sticky plastic jelly shoes, and ran down to the end of the rough-hewn wooden dock. Just as I squished through some of the fallen mulberries, someone called out a warning. They said that the lake had been drained and not to jump off the deck. Drained? Who "drains" a lake? Absurd! I ignored this odd comment and jumped into the cold water, feet first.

In the ER later that morning, a cadre of nurses held me down as a physician removed several pebbles that had embedded themselves deep under the skin of my right heel.

Fourteen years later, at a more worldly twenty-six years of age, yet another impetuous leap would end my career, nearly end my life, and bring my world crashing down.

We moved around a lot when I was growing up. Chicago, Evanston, Northbrook, Glenview, Oak Park, Bolingbrook, and other parts of the greater Chicago area were all home for a bit. In late 1986, we moved with our mom to Maryland, while she was stationed at Aberdeen Proving Grounds for her Officer Basic Course (OBC).

That move was a rude awakening. Oak Park, Illinois had felt like a melting pot, a place where people from different ethnic, cultural, and financial backgrounds interacted and made it work. Our friends down the street and members of our extended family were Black, and that was normal. That's the way our mother raised us. My best friends in elementary school were from diverse backgrounds. They were Hispanic, Asian, Jewish, Hindu, Christian, Muslim, or Buddhist, but I knew them only as friends. We would adjust sleepover menus to fit everyone's needs and find common ground. We all learned to enjoy the unique food and culture each of us brought to the group. Different was normal and good—it meant an opportunity to learn and grow.

That was not the case in Maryland. There, my sister and I were slotted into rigid categories. We were white students in a seventy percent Black school. Friend groups at our new school were separated by skin color, religion, and financial status. As we waited for a bus to school on the first day, we were pelted by rocks thrown by Black students. At school, a group of girls threatened to beat my sister up because of her blond hair, blue eyes, and pale complexion. The intolerance was considered to be a given, and "just the way things are" by the school administrators. Our mom did what she could and tried to make it work. But when it was clear that our safety would be an ongoing concern, she moved us out to a more rural and predominately white area of Maryland.

Feeling judged based on my appearance for that fleeting moment in time changed the way I view others. It sharpened my resolve to see everyone as an individual. Racism is horrific and unacceptable. It's impossible for me to ever really know what it is like to be the victim of racism. I can not imagine what it's like to live with unsubstantiated bias every moment of everyday. What must it feel like to know that the very systems put in place to educate, care for, or protect us are causing undue harm?

We were privileged enough to have the option to simply move. We stayed with our mom's childhood friend Rae Ann and her family. Rae Ann, her husband, Warren, and their children lived an hour or so from Aberdeen Proving Ground. My sister and I went to school with their children in Westminster, Maryland. The commute to base was longer, as was the bus ride to our new school. But we felt more comfortable and no one tried to stone us.

On the weekends, Mom brought us back to base to make arts and crafts, ceramics, and small woodworking projects through the Morale, Welfare, and Recreation department (MWR). We ate dinner at the officers' club when we could, which afforded a beautiful view of the Chesapeake Bay. Upon Mom's graduation from Officer Basic Course (OBC), we headed back to the Chicago area.

15
JEAN: ASSUMPTIONS

IN 1988, WE MOVED BACK to the Chicagoland area and the suburb of Riverside, Illinois, where I started my freshman year at Riverside-Brookfield High School. Again, I felt uncomfortable with the lack of diversity and acceptance. Riverside was predominately white and Christian. I befriended someone who was Jewish, but who tried to keep her religion a secret. Another friend was from a Greek Orthodox family, but she went by a very plain Americanized name rather than by her Greek given name.

At lunch one day I heard someone use the n-word, and was floored! I have always been outspoken against racism, sexism, and other isms. When someone used a racial slur, I called them out on it. One of my fellow students took to printing a photo of me with a drawing of a swastika on my forehead. Why a swastika? Was it because I had a Jewish friend? Because I sometimes had matzah in my lunch? I have no idea. He posted the photos throughout our school and threatened ongoing harassment. He said he would stop if I paid him. I informed him that it was blackmail, and that I would happily contact the police. He eventually gave up.

I was raised to see people for who they are at heart, not what they look like. The thought of looking down on someone because of their race or religion was not a concept I could comprehend. Intolerance was not something I could stomach. Whether it was a matter of changing with whom I sat with at lunch, or alternating what I did during my study hall to avoid other students, I tried to separate myself from the outspoken racists in my school.

As a new student, and being new to the area, I had no friends at the start of the school year. Things were made even more uncomfortable for me by a really bad haircut and a head cold. Yes, a completely unsuitable and very boyish haircut. My aunt Linda, who was in cosmetology school at the time, thought it would be great to give me a wedge cut. This essentially meant that she shaved the back of my head, and the rest of my hair was cut to look like I had a triangle shaped head. It did not suit me, and was made even worse by my very curly hair. In the end, it looked more like a mushroom or bowl cut. Rather than something fun and youthful, it was boyish and unflattering on me.

My first day in Spanish language class, I sat in the back and hoped to blend in. Unfortunately, a girl at the front of the class stood up and said that I looked just like the boy on the cover of the book she was reading. The book was then passed around so that everyone could compare my boyish haircut with that of the drawing. I didn't know that she was talking about me until someone sitting in front of me turned around and loudly stated, "I thought you were a girl." Yes, I am a girl. But at that time, I was a meek girl with an achingly bad haircut.

To further confound my classmates and ensure that I would not have a high school boyfriend, I misunderstood a question another student asked me in a science class later that day. I had a head cold, stuffy nose, and sore throat, and still had difficulty processing auditory information. When she asked if I was a "homo," I thought she was asking if my species was *homo sapiens*.

Never having heard the term "homo" used in any other way, it being a science class after all, and being way too shy to ask for further clarification, I thought I was simply verifying that we were all smart, science-focused people who referred to ourselves as *homo sapiens*, not just humans. So I said yes, and I am fairly certain that everyone in my high school still thinks that I'm gay, which I am not.

High school was a difficult time for me. Unfortunately, I was a terrible student. I could do extremely well on exams, especially in math and science, but I earned mediocre grades. I abhorred homework. Unless it was something particularly interesting or challenging, I rarely, if ever, handed in assignments. It didn't help that I continued to have difficulty processing auditory information.

I guess I've always had rather low self-esteem and social anxiety, which didn't help dig me out of the hole of social isolation. My default has been not to try hard. This way, I wasn't really failing at something, I was just not trying hard enough.

Although joining the military was never really something I talked about with my family, when my high school offered the Armed Services Vocational Aptitude Battery (ASVAB), I took it. I liked science and helping people, so I thought that I might want to pursue a career in medicine. My mom's friend Alex, her high school math teacher, suggested that I should give medicine a trial run. Alex had gone to medical school and then realized that he did not want to be a physician. He went back to school and became a teacher. Alex was a fantastic math teacher, and he tutored my sister and me. I grew up loving mathematical proofs and solving logic puzzles, all thanks to Alex. So when he suggested that I work as a medic for the National Guard to try my hand at medicine, I agreed.

The military would provide me with the training and opportunity to work as a combat medic while I worked toward my college degree. If it turned out that I was not suited for a career in medicine, then I would know by the time I was a college sophomore and had completed my basic education college courses.

Two or so weeks after completing the ASVAB, my guidance counselor informed me that we would receive our test results and meet with the recruiter. I called my mom, just to let her know that the results were back, and she hightailed it over from the local National Guard Armory in North Riverside, Illinois. My high school was small, 400 or so students in all, and only about 90 in my grade level. Only a handful of students had taken the exam, and we met in the school's small conference room. Although I was not a great student, academically, I wasn't a "trouble maker," and my counselor had never met my mother. My mom arrived in uniform, a woodland green camouflage battle dress outfit, with her new remarried name, Tomas, stitched above one shirt pocket.

When my mother and stepfather had married the year before, my sister and I kept our father's last name. We did this more for a sense of continuity than any feeling of loyalty. So, I, Jean Marie Elizabeth McNamara, sat at one end of the conference table with my mother Lita Tomas's arm around my shoulder as we looked over my ASVAB test results. The other students, all male, gave us funny looks, as did my counselor and the recruiter. I chalked this up to my being the only girl thinking about joining the military. But I was wrong. Apparently, they all thought my mother was a female recruiter who was sexually harassing me! Because of the name difference and probably in part because I look more like my very tall, dark-haired biological father than my petite blonde haired mother, they did not make an immediate connection. It didn't help that my mother never, ever, introduces herself. Not at parties, not at military events, not when someone stops her on the street to say "Hi," not even on the telephone. She just rolls right into a conversation. That is something which still drives me crazy to this day.

I didn't really understand my ASVAB test results, and they were never really clearly explained. How could test results be higher than one hundred points? My mom, however, seemed pleased, and gave me a hug. She said that according to the test, I could do anything I wanted in the military.

As we were leaving the conference room, I called out, "Mom!" to get her attention and heard a group gasp and a number of whispered exclamations.

One of the boys next to me said, "Oh, she's your mom!"

My counselor laughed and added, "For a minute there, I thought you were being harassed by a recruiter." All I could think was: *of course she's my mom, and if you thought I was being harassed, why didn't you say something?*

All bizarre high school experiences and misunderstandings aside, I joined the Army for a myriad of reasons. In part, my family influenced my decision. My mother, maternal grandfather, maternal step-grandfather, great uncles, stepfather, and one paternal uncle all served in the military. My maternal grandmother, stepfather, and one of my paternal uncles all worked for the U.S. government. So my family and its service to this country molded my view of the military and the U.S. government. I grew up believing that we all needed to do our part. This added weight and support to my decision to join the Illinois Army National Guard.

Mom, an S4 logistics officer, had already been discussing me, her new recruit, with the other members of the 108th Support Battalion staff. So when we walked into the battalion office, we stopped to talk with the G1, who controlled the personnel and basically acted as the head human resource officer.

I had met the G1, Major Sue Maas, once before. She and her husband were both in the military, and had a young family in Riverside. During the 1991 riots in Chicago, following the Chicago Bulls Championship win, Major Maas and her husband had had to report to their respective National Guard units in the middle of the night. I volunteered to babysit for their children.

Upon request, Major Maas was kind enough to go through the 108th Modification Table of Organization and Equipment (MTOE), or manning roster. She found several positions for which I qualified based on my scores on the ASVAB. I already had my sights on a position as a medic, and with everything in order, I signed on as the newest member of Charlie Company, 108th Support Battalion, Thirty-Third Brigade. My training was scheduled to begin the fall after my high school graduation.

Between my junior and senior years in high school, I took two leadership courses with Hosteling International (HI). The first trip was a quick local training session at the University of Chicago campus. We stayed in dorm rooms and were trained to budget for a group trip, basic first aid, and other tasks a trip leader might need. The next trip was a bit longer. It was a more advanced and intensive leadership course held while hiking along the Appalachian Trail. It was akin to on-the-job training. While hiking the Appalachian Trail, I learned about group dynamics, backcountry navigating with a compass, map reading, trip planning and budgeting, emergency medicine, and "leave no trace behind" principles. I was by far the youngest and most naïve member of the group. Talks around the fireplace about drugs and sex went right over my head. I think my mother and I used those trips as a litmus test, thinking if I could handle hiking along the Appalachian Trail, then maybe I could survive military basic training.

When I graduated from high school, I took one more trip with HI. I had applied for a grant that would pay for an extensive hiking trip throughout Europe, but was turned down. Instead, my mother graciously paid for me to take an HI led trip around Mont Blanc, the highest mountain in the Alps.

The night before the trip, my sister handed me a mixtape and five dollars. She said the mixtape was in case I felt homesick. The five dollars was for flowers she wanted me to leave on the grave of Jim Morrison, my sister's favorite singer.

When I landed in Paris, I was very tired and jet lagged. I went to the closest hostel, and was informed that there was no space available. These were the days before everyone had a cellular telephone. The hostel staff gave me a list of potential local hotels, and I set out. After finding a room with a shared bathroom down the hall, I went out to explore the City of Light. This was my first trip abroad on my own and I was very lucky that the people of Paris were extremely kind and patient with me. These were also the days before digital photography. My mom had lent me her Canon Rebel, a bevy of heavy lenses, and thirty rolls of film. Not thinking how expensive developing all of that film would be, I snapped away.

Before heading to the Alps and my hiking trip, I stopped at a small flower shop outside the gates of the cemetery where Jim Morrison was laid to rest. The florist there was an old man. I paid for a red rose, and turned to leave when the florist grabbed my arm and restrained me. He tried to pull me behind a curtain and into his living quarters. I pulled away, while pretending to call out to a nonexistent friend outside. I'm not sure what he wanted, but I was happy to get away from him. After that, I wanted to get out of the city and join up with my hiking tour group. I took a train to Chamonix, the Alps, and adventure. As someone who had taken four years of Spanish, and was rather shy, I faced a few challenges.

All in all, the trip was thrilling and confidence-building. When I returned to Chicago, the world looked different to me. I was a bit less shy and more self-assured. My next trip would be even more transformative. I was headed to Basic Training and a new career.

16

JEAN: BASIC TRAINING FOR BLACK SHEEP

BEFORE HEADING TO BASIC TRAINING, I had to return to the Military Entrance Processing Station (MEPS). They wanted everyone with an appointment at MEPS to be there first thing in the morning, and we were all required to stay at a nearby hotel the night before.

After checking in at the front desk, I proceeded to my room. I was surprised to find that I would be sharing a room. My roommate was already in the room, and she had spilled water from an iron all over one bed. She was sleeping comfortably in the dry bed. She seemed very nervous about the upcoming medical evaluation, and spoke at a rapid clip.

Apparently, she was worried about the urinalysis part of her upcoming physical, as she had used illegal drugs in the past. She had placed a small brown glass bottle on the bedside table. She said it contained a liquid that she believed would help her pass the drug test. When I told her that I knew nothing about drugs, she left the room and went outside to smoke. I'm not sure what happened to her or if she passed her drug screening. I took the wet blankets off the bed, brought them to the front desk, and exchanged them for dry linens. Then I went straight to sleep. My roommate and the wet bed were the least of my worries.

The dreaded scale worried me! At nineteen years old, I was five foot six and 149 pounds, right on the cusp of the upper weight limit for enlistment. I had worked at a health club, taught group fitness classes, and lifted weights on a regular basis during high school. At home, I had run on a treadmill. But I hadn't seen the results I wanted.

Although I was never fat as a child, I was never skinny either. I have wide hips and shoulders and a relatively small waist. As far back as I can remember, my thighs have met in the middle, without a gap. I've always enjoyed food, at times to excess! Cans of soda, bowls of fettuccine al burro, deep-dish Chicago-style pizza, Hungarian goulash, vanilla custard ice cream, chocolate cream pie, and oversized bowls of sugary cereal built those thighs.

After my initial appointment at a MEPS and my entry physical months before, I had switched to lean proteins, salads, lots of vegetables, and water. In addition to extra running and trips to the gym I tried more desperate measures to ensure that I would weigh-in. I even tried body wraps that were lauded for taking inches off your hips. From my ankles to my waist, a spa technician wrapped me up like a mummy in heavy elastic bandages soaked in a warm liquid clay. This treatment might have helped for the day at least. The night before I was to ship out, I had skipped dinner, and the next morning, I passed on breakfast, too, to make sure I would pass the weigh-in.

Perhaps due to nerves, perhaps due to a lack of food, I do not recall my flight from Chicago O'Hare airport to Fort Jackson for basic training at all. The next thing I remember, I was in South Carolina and checking in at the United Service Organization (USO) center inside the airport.

A couple of drill sergeants rounded up all of us new recruits from the USO and loaded us onto a bus for the thirty-minute ride to Fort Jackson.

That night, in the reception area, I slept in a modern open bay barracks filled with bunk beds and fifty or so other new recruits. The next day, I shuffled through the different stations to get my gear.

The Army supplied us with nearly everything we would need for the next two months: towels, PT uniforms (which doubled as pajamas), boots, socks, a laundry bag, a coat, gloves, a rain poncho, a canteen for water, T-shirts, uniforms (both summer and winter weight), and de rigueur luggage of an olive drab bag with our name painted on to haul it all in. We also received a thick pocket-sized manual, or Field Manual (FM) 21-13, The Soldier's Field Guide, which detailed everything we would learn during basic training. They even provide eyeglasses, commonly known as Birth Control Glasses, or BCGs. The eyeglass frames are universally loathed and mocked for their ugliness. No one looks good in them.

After receiving all of my gear, I headed outside and joined the hundreds of other female recruits. It felt a bit surreal knowing that I was going through the exact same things, and in the exact same place, that my mom had before me. It felt a bit like a right of passage, or like another sacrament, but with hand grenades and semi-automatic weapons.

With our duffles at our feet, we waited while the drill sergeants picked out who would be in which platoons. I was assigned to a platoon nicknamed the "Black Sheep," which sounded rather ominous to me. But then again, I guess I've always felt like a bit of a Black Sheep.

We were loaded into the back of a military transport vehicle and headed to Tank Hill. At the time, I thought Tank Hill referred to Army tanks, and that the barracks sat on a hill. An Army base area referred to as Tank Hill—that made sense. Years later, I would learn that it actually referred to an elevated water storage tank at the top of the hill, which has since been removed.

For the next two months, my home away from home was one of the same World War II-era barracks my mom had stayed in during her basic training. Mine was one of many sturdy, old, wood-clad, two-floor buildings, one for each platoon, that dotted the hill, with bunks and a bathroom on each floor. At the entrance was a storage locker where we all placed our civilian luggage, which we wouldn't see again for two months. The only items not issued by the Army, and still not issued today, were our base layers. We had to bring our own underwear and brassieres with us or purchase them at the Fort Jackson Base Exchange. I got a few sports bras for everyday use and one more traditional brassiere for wearing with my dress uniform or Class As. My mom had purchased my underwear for me because of the way they rolled up nice for display in a foot locker, not for style. They were huge plain white cotton underwear. My brown Army issued t-shirts reached almost down to my knees and my granny panties reached all the way up to my rib cage. I was encased in fabric.

Soon I learned that my basic training was to be a bit atypical. The drill sergeants were reservists, part of the Provisional Roundout Training (PROTRAIN) program. Every two weeks, we got a new cadre of drill instructors as they cycled through their annual training.

Each group would come in hard charging! We would start all over again with the in-your face screaming drill sergeant phase. Near the end of the two-week period, the staff would relax a little, as they had had enough time to get to know us as individuals. Then the new cadre would roll in, full of spit and vinegar.

Our mess hall was at the end of the block of barracks, a small one-story building arranged perpendicular to the line of barracks. There, I learned to peel buckets full of potatoes with a dull butter knife while on Kitchen Police (KP) duty.

At night, we each had to take turns on "Fire Guard," sitting between the bathroom and bunks, under the overhead light that illuminated the staircase. We were there to pull the fire alarm and wake everyone up if there was a fire, suicide attempt, or other emergency. We could also quickly locate our fellow soldier's bunks if anyone received an emergency message from home, relayed by the American Red Cross, in the middle of the night. For most of us, Fire Guard was our chance to meditate and write home.

Mom had packed two letters in my bag before I left home for basic training. One envelope read, "Open when you graduate." The other read, "Open if you do not graduate. It will be ok."

I had not prepared adequately for basic training, despite the plethora of resources available to me. I ought to have gotten into better physical shape. At the end of each day, running to and from different classes and up and down stairs in combat boots, my shins ached. The pain was so bad that I often whimpered as I climbed the barracks stairs and up to my bunk. The stress and increased physical activity meant that I didn't have a menstrual cycle for four months, two in Basic Training and the first two of AIT.

After eight weeks of daily PT, I was in better shape, but I still had a weak upper body and difficulty with push-ups. Did you know that there's a proper way to do a push-up to prevent injury? I did not! Apparently, I did push-ups the wrong way, and my wrists were very weak, which only added to my physical pain. Twenty years later I would learn that I have a connective tissue disorder, which may have hastened my shin and wrist damage and pain.

One day, my platoon was standing around talking in small groups outside the barracks, waiting for formation. I saw the gleam of brass on someone walking toward us. Instead of simply saluting the officer as an individual, I called the platoon to attention and stood in front of the group. The officer walked up to me and asked me what I was going to do now. I had no idea what to do. So, I did a really dumb thing! I ordered, "Present arms." Dear Lord, what was I thinking? He laughed and walked away. I waited to see if the ground would open up and swallow me whole! As red as a beet, I turned back to the platoon, said, "Order arms" and "Fall out." I was not ready to lead a platoon!

This was my first experience living in close quarters with a bunch of strangers. The Army attempted to prevent the spread of illness by giving everyone a booster shot the first week of Basic, along with a plethora of immunizations. Unfortunately, not long after arriving at Ft. Jackson, I got extremely sick. My throat felt a little scratchy one day, and the next day I sounded like a squeaky mouse. After a week, my throat was on fire! I could hardly swallow and was feverish. I went on sick call and a medic gave me a bottle of huge orange 800-milligram ibuprofen, known colloquially as "horse pills" or "Ranger candy."

After another week without relief, I begrudgingly went on sick call again. I was terrified that I was going to miss out on some vital training, would be "recycled," and would have to start Basic Training over again. Again I saw a medic, not a physician, nurse, or PA. This was someone who had had four months of basic medical training. He had some help, a small flow chart of symptoms and treatments. He flipped through a small binder to "sore throat," and read the information. He then reached into a desk drawer full of small packages of throat lozenges. He never looked in my throat or even checked my temperature.

Unsurprisingly, by the next week, I was feeling even worse. Again, I went to sick call, and again, I received a package of lozenges. My drill instructors took pity on me and exempted me from the NBCR (nuclear, biological, chemical, or radiological) tear gas training. I also had terrible shin splints. But at sick call, they would only treat one health problem per visit. So I continued to run in my combat boots and consequently to this day I have painful lumps of scar tissue along each of my shins.

With the rest of the platoon, I qualified with an M16A1 rifle, stabbed a straw-filled dummy with a bayonet, climbed to the top of the confidence course tower and rappelled back down, and fulfilled all of the other requirements to pass basic. My platoon learned to march together in-step and respond quickly to basic drill and ceremony commands. After graduating from Basic, I was on my way to AIT, in Texas.

Unfortunately, I was still sick and hoarse when I flew from South Carolina to San Antonio, Texas. On the flight, I opened both of the letters from my mom. I wasn't all that surprised to find that both the "Congratulations, you've made it through Basic" and the "Sorry, the Army's not for you" letters were identical. My mom simply said that she'd always been proud of me, and that no matter what, I would make my stamp on the world. She knew what it was like to go through Basic training, and that it was mentally and physically challenging. I appreciated her thoughtful and pragmatic approach, covering all the bases and being supportive either way.

I arrived at my new training unit a few days before the rest of my new platoon. My barracks was in a new modern brick building. All of the women in my company were housed in one building across a walkway from an identical building for all of the men. A small building attached to the male barracks contained the company headquarters. After checking in with HQ, I was directed to wait by the covered assembly area and told someone would come by to show me to my bunk.

I spotted a small group of young men and women in civilian clothes sitting on the ground, polishing their combat boots. I introduced myself and learned that they were holdovers from the previous class. They had not passed either the written or physical exams and were set to be discharged. They seemed happy and relaxed. They told me that they were allowed to keep the T-shirts, socks, towels, and boots they'd been issued in basic training. They sat there talking and joking, all while still polishing their boots. I was not quite sure what to make of that group. Would the training be so horrible that a person could be happy to go home with only a small collection of items to show for it? Why were they still polishing their boots?

AIT was more mentally and physically challenging than basic training. We had to learn basic anatomy, physiology, triage, and phlebotomy. We were taught all of the things one needed to qualify as an emergency medical technician (EMT) at the basic level. Our job would be to keep someone alive long enough to get them to a field hospital. For some, the stress was far too much.

One of my fellow classmates swallowed an entire bottle of ibuprofen in a suicide attempt. Another decorated a bathroom stall with used feminine products and feces. Both were quickly discharged from service.

My days at Fort Sam were physically challenging, and the coursework was tough, but there was less yelling and more actual instruction. With nothing short of trepidation, I checked the exam result posting each week. My insecurities told me that I had not done well and would fail out of class, but I was wrong. As I looked for my id number and test score I was shocked to see that I ranked third academically in my class. After all, my squad leader was a trained nurse and my platoon sergeant was a guy in his thirties with two PhDs.

The man with the two PhDs was given the rank of E-4, or specialist, because of his advanced degrees. He was put in charge of our platoon, but I soon learned that intelligence and education do not make you a leader. He did not know how to delegate, talk with people (especially women), or handle stressful situations.

At AIT, we were granted more freedom, including weekend passes off post. I had been to San Antonio once before, with my mother, and was familiar with the San Antonio River Walk and a few of the local restaurants. A group of us often headed into town to see the sights, take time to actually chew our food, wear civilian clothes, and try not to walk in step with one another.

I had a crush on one of my platoon's squad leaders. We never had a chance to get to know each other, however. He collapsed one day and was hospitalized due to a spontaneous hemopneumothorax.

After he was discharged from the Army, I started hanging out with his battle buddy, another squad leader, who was born in Okinawa, Japan, and raised in California. Please do not think I'm fickle! I did not simply jump from one crush to the next.

I first truly noticed him one afternoon when I was sitting on the covered cement patio outside my Fort Sam Houston barracks. That day, the man whom I'll call "Cali" sat down next to me. He scooped up a handful of the wet sand at my feet and proceeded to form it into tiny graduated cubes and spheres.

As someone who grew up around the artistically talented, I think I'm the only one in my family who cannot draw, but I adore art! This simple act of forming a collection of clean, elegant sand sculptures piqued my interest in this quiet young man. I was soon enamored by his goofy running style and his artistic flair. Cali wooed me, and he was very good at wooing.

We spent hours talking. He taught me about his Japanese-Italian background, and spent time really getting to know me. He was also easy on the eyes. At just over six feet tall, he was a bit lanky, but he was fit. His skin was a tawny golden brown, which made his smile all the brighter. A year younger than me, he sported a high and tight crewcut, and whiskey-colored eyes that drank in the light.

Over the course of the next few months in Texas, Cali and I spent an increasing amount of our free time together. Since we were allowed to go off post on the weekends, we explored San Antonio and the River Walk. We were young and physically fit. Our hormones had been building up over the prior eight weeks, and it wasn't long before we were in a hotel room together. We spent entire weekends in bed together.

After we graduated from AIT, our future together was rather uncertain. I returned to my home in Illinois, and he returned to his home in California. When I arrived at my house, however, a dozen roses from him waited for me on my doorstep.

We spent long hours on the phone, and as these were the days before instant communication, we wrote a flurry of letters back and forth. Yes, we actually mailed handwritten letters, on paper, with stamps and everything, via the United States Post Office. Cali also sent me countless bouquets of flowers and other small gifts, each with a thoughtful card. Although I thought we had fun, I did not think our relationship would outlast AIT. But within a year, Cali had moved to Illinois, into my home, my National Guard Unit, and my college.

One class we both decided to take was a basic, one-credit fitness class. Four or so days a week, we'd head to the fitness center and complete a circuit of weight and cardio exercises. It was a good way to stay in shape. To get an "A," we also had to go to the library, watch a few fitness or health-related videos from a designated list, and take a related quiz.

One day, we picked a VHS video about preventing back injuries. We picked up the video and walked over to a line of TV/VCR players that the library had set up to watch such educational videos. We donned our headphones and sat side by side to watch. The video started normally, with cartoon characters demonstrating both improper and proper bending and lifting techniques. Then this "health" video took an unexpected turn. In the middle of our school library, we sat there, mouths agape, cheeks aflame, and giggles bubbling in our throats as a cartoon couple began having sex. We sat there watching the cartoons use different props and sexual positions meant to prevent back injuries and back strain.

I was so embarrassed! Cali, however, turned to me and said, "Let's watch that again!"

17

JEAN: LONG NAILS AND RUSTY FORCEPS

BECAUSE OF MY DESIRE TO help people, I had specifically joined the Charlie Company (C Company) part of the 108th Support Battalion, in Illinois Army National. It was close to home, I could still go to college, and the National Guard would help pay for my tuition and books. Since I was considering a career in medicine, I thought that working as a medic would give me a feel for the medical career field.

My unit was stationed at the North Riverside Armory, off of Cermak Road, just north of the Brookfield Zoological Society and a four-minute drive from my home in Brookfield. My mom was at that time the company commander for Bravo Company. Her office and headquarters was only one door down the hall from my company's headquarters. We could even carpool to weekend drill.

In a weird coincidence two of her full time staff members shared the same first names as my sister and I: "Jean and Kim." It kind of felt like her command there was fated. During the week she was "mom" when I would visit her at her office in the Armory, bringing her coffee or lunch. However, on drill weekends, she was no longer "mom," she was "ma'am" and I would have to salute her. Although, I did slip on more than one occasion and call her mom, which garnered shocked stares from anyone nearby.

My unit, C Company, was divided into two factions: the ambulance platoon and the treatment platoon. Although in theory the two platoons should have worked well together, with the ambulance platoon transporting the sick and injured to the treatment platoon for care, in practice a great deal of animosity existed between the two platoons.

I had thought that the ambulance platoon, being the baby of the full-time NCO, would receive more mission critical training. After talking with Cali, who was assigned to that platoon, I learned that no one in our company was receiving the training or testing I had expected. Everyone acted as an individual, not as a unit. It wasn't what I was raised to expect from a military unit. It wasn't what I had hoped it would be. I wanted to be a part of an Army unit that worked together to accomplish a goal or mission!

From what I could see, no one enforced uniform regulations in Charlie Company. The full-time supply sergeant and several of her subordinates grew their nails so long that they began to curl under. Their nails were also highly decorative, painted with designs in multiple colors and adorned with rhinestones. And many of the men in the unit, including my platoon sergeant, sported long pinky finger nails. No matter the reasons for growing nails that long, they were not regulation length. Also, it's hard to check someone's capillary refill rate when their nails are coated with dark lacquer.

More egregious was the blatant lying and cheating my superiors considered par for the course. I watched while my platoon sergeant helped people cheat on weapons qualification. He would use a pen cap, apparently the same size as a bullet hole, to poke through the paper targets. I also watched while high ranking officers cheated on the Army Physical Fitness Test. They would lay with their bellies on the ground and barely move their arms as though they were doing push-ups. I found myself growing more and more disenfranchised and apathetic toward the Illinois Army National Guard. It wasn't the bastion of morals and honor that I was looking for and wanted to be a part of.

When I joined the unit, the company commander was working for a toy store rather than in a medical field in his day-to-day career.

From day one, I felt that the full-time training NCO, Sgt. M, despised me. I was a headstrong and enthusiastic new recruit, and something about me must have grated on him. I was always early for drill weekend, happy to volunteer for extra duty, and totally clueless. The unit, in contrast, had an extremely laid back and relaxed vibe. I've never been a laid back or relaxed person. I'm an uptight, play by the rules, do your job and go home type of person. I was a poor fit for the unit. I like rules and regulations. They exist for a reason!

Prior to shipping out for Basic Training and AIT I attended several drill weekends. One of my first assigned tasks was typing up forms, in triplicate. These were the somewhat antiquated forms with carbon paper between each sheet. There was no way to correct errors as they would be made in triplicate. I don't type. Our first typewriter at home was digital, followed shortly by a computer. So, it was a very long day of my hunting and pecking for letters on the typewriter, making mistakes, and having to start all over again. I think that my sergeant may have thought my ineptitude was a form of insubordination. I would have been far happier, and more qualified, to clean the latrines. The sergeant would stalk back and forth between his office and the bullpen, sighing loudly and demanding to know if I was finished.

It may have annoyed him that I would visit my mom during the week, passing his office on the way to my mother's office down the hall.

Each summer, my National Guard battalion spent two weeks

for annual training (AT) in the woods at Fort McCoy, near LaCrosse, Wisconsin, the land of the prolific deer tick. These ticks covered the trunks of the trees, making it look as though the bark was crawling. They would then drop off and onto those unwitting enough to walk past. I will never lean or sit against a tree without carefully checking it's bark for ticks first. The ticks were everywhere on Fort McCoy. Someone would go to use the latrine and end up with a tick on their ass or other private areas, and as a medic it was my job to remove these ticks and send them in for testing. Lyme disease was a real concern.

Since I was a medic with a medical company and treatment platoon, I spent my annual training jotting down SOAP notes (an outline of subjective symptoms, objective signs, assessment or diagnosis, and plan of treatment), starting IVs, removing ticks, and taking vitals. We set up a field hospital, comprised of three tents, in a heavily wooded area, and started treating the basic injuries and ailments that befell our fellow guardsmen. Based on what I witnessed, a number of people in our battalion used our presence at annual training to take care of all of their healthcare needs. I saw more cases of chronic foot fungal infections and old injuries than one would have expected.

For the rest of the year, I was a college student, and did not practice any of these tasks, so the first few IVs each summer, typically for dehydrated soldiers, were always rough! It took time for the technique to come back to me, and the patients requiring an IV suffered as a result. If it was something we practiced each month, during drill weekends, or even quarterly I think things would have been different. It would always take a while to get back into the swing of my SOAP note format and recall basic medical terminology. The physicians and physician assistant on staff, though, were amazing! They always made a concerted effort to reeducate and guide those of us unaccustomed to treating patients in the civilian world on a day-to-day basis.

The rest of the year, my platoon performed physicals. We spent no time training or preparing for annual training or our wartime mission. Instead, we collected urine samples, ran hearing tests, recorded height and weight, and conducted a basic vision screening. On drill weekends, we did not review the emergency medical care or techniques that could potentially save lives at AT. There were no classes or a review of basic first aid, medical evacuation procedures, how to treat patients in an NBCR environment, biohazard procedures, phlebotomy, ambulance procedures, triage, mental health care and emergencies, how to write up SOAP notes, or any of the other things that could have made the medics in my company efficient and effective at patient care during annual training or at war. Additionally, the monthly drill was always a bit awkward. Some months, only two or three soldiers from my platoon were in attendance. I never heard from my squad leader, and I rarely saw my platoon sergeant except when he was smoking, and therefore stood out.

My platoon leader was never with our platoon while we performed physicals during monthly drill, and was rarely seen at annual training. For the two weeks each summer when we were at Fort McCoy, my squad leader stayed in a cot, complaining of back pain, taking muscle relaxants, and offering little to no guidance.

That is except for when she reprimanded me for throwing a dirty paper in a bag of regular trash instead of putting it in with the recycling. I was adamant about recycling before it was trendy, and had even volunteered at a recycling center while in high school. To the best of my knowledge you can not recycle a soiled paper plate. But all the same, it gave her a chance to belittle me in front of our platoon.

I have always been headstrong. I felt that we should do our best in every situation and help one another. I would question orders that were contrary to the rules and regulations and everything I'd been taught and believed in. If a patient was in need of extended or specialty care, for which we were not equipped, I felt they should be treated at the Base or community hospital, and not in a tent in the middle of the forest by inexperienced medics. If someone bled all over the wool blanket that covered their cot, I felt that blanket should be considered a biohazard, and sent out for cleaning! The blankets were reused rather than being changed between patients, and they were packed away at the end of the two weeks, to be used again the next year. Although Sgt. M insisted that he sent them out for cleaning, they were exactly where we had put them the year before. With the exact same stains, the occasional dead insect, and a deeper musty scent.

For field hospitals, nothing much had changed since the Korean War. We would set up a General Purpose (GP) large olive drab (OD) green hospital tent. The 18' wide by 52' long canvas structure was partitioned into six exam areas with rope and hanging wool OD green blankets screening one area from the next. Canvas cots were set up as exam tables. At the entrance of the tent was a field desk across from a weapons rack. No weapons were permitted beyond the entrance of the hospital tent. Behind the main treatment tent was a ward tent, for those requiring overnight care, a dental tent, and a sleeping tent for the company. In the field, where hand washing was an infrequent event at best, contagious illness spread like wildfire. We had one handwashing station in the treatment tent and one by the mess area.

Once, a Colonel with pink eye came to me for treatment. I was surprised to see he was still in the field, as I thought for health concerns anyone with pink eye would be sent back to the barracks. As I watched him rub his eye with his right hand and then go right back to jotting notes in his notebook, I cringed. I stared at his pen in horror! If he continued to touch things that other people might also use we were going to see a lot more cases of pink eye. I put a bandage over his eye and reminded him to wash his hands frequently and leave his eye alone. But it was far too late, and we were inundated with more and more cases of conjunctivitis.

As I walked from the triage tent to the mess area for lunch another day, I passed an ambulance with its motor running. Glancing into the driver's compartment through the front windshield, I noticed that there wasn't anyone there. *Who would leave a vehicle running?* My curiosity got the better of me, and I walked around to the back of the ambulance and threw open the back doors.

Inside was a very pale young man on a cot. He was shivering and what looked like a bag of blood was connected to his IV line. I was confused, as we didn't have blood in the field. Anyone needing a blood transfusion would presumably be medivaced to a nearby hospital. *So, what on earth was going on?* I thought. *What was wrong with this patient? Why wasn't he being processed through to the treatment platoon for treatment? Where in the hell were the medics assigned to this ambulance? Was this some sort of weird test?*

As I stood there, my mouth agape, a second lieutenant walked up. He informed me that he and the man on the cot were both platoon leaders for another company. His friend had gotten bitten by a tick and then started having flu-like symptoms. I leaned down and noticed that the bite mark was now ringed with a bullseye rash.

The man continued, informing me that the ambulance platoon sergeant, my bête noire Sgt. M, had decided that the patient should stay in the back of the air conditioned ambulance and on an IV bag of lactated Ringer's solution to help him "recover."

At this, I realized that the patient had been left alone for so long that his IV bag had run dry and refilled with his own blood! I was utterly dumbfounded. *What in the world was a patient doing in the back of an ambulance by himself? Who could leave someone alone like that?* As a unit, we should have been practicing for real life scenarios like this during the rest of the year. If we all knew what to do, in particular how we should cycle medics out for breaks, meals, and rest periods, then a patient would never have been left alone.

When the medics and Sgt. M returned, they all said I was overreacting. *Was I? What if the patient had tried to get up? What if in his fevered delirium he had wandered off into the woods? What if he had to go to the bathroom?* I was incredulous and rather vocal about my disapproval. In my opinion the patient ought to have been transported to the hospital, given the appropriate antibiotics, and our unit should have taken a good look at the gaping holes in our treatment protocols.

In the end the man in the ambulance stopped to thank me on his way back to his unit. There was more color in his cheeks and his fever was gone. I can only hope that he wasn't traumatized by his experience or later debilitated by Lyme disease.

Although it may seem that a simple two weeks away from home camping in the woods of Wisconsin wasn't a big deal, there were always countless injuries and illnesses to treat. Someone's life could be forever changed if we didn't know what we were doing, acted too slowly, or dropped the ball in the continuity of care.

One day, a female soldier arrived at the treatment tent needing care for a badly burned hand. She had been removing a trip flare, which is a flare mounted to a tree with a tripwire extending from it. If someone unfamiliar with the area walks by, snagging or tripping over the outstretched line, the flare ignites alerting everyone of an intruder.

A flare is hot! They are said to burn at temperatures above 2,000 degrees fahrenheit. Apparently she was holding the flare while disabling the trip line. Somehow the flare ignited and burned her hand.

I saw a number of burns while in the field at AT. Another soldier burned her hand on the stock of an M60 machine gun that had just been fired. Although her burns weren't as bad, as the barrel can get hot but only up to around 300 or so degrees, they were still avoidable. After debriding their wounds, in a bowl of ice water and iodine, I passed their care on to one of the physicians.

One more burn patient sticks out in my mind. He was shot at very close range in the crotch by a blank round. A blank is round that gives you the bang and flash of a regular round, but with paper instead of lead shot. They can still be very dangerous and even deadly at close range. Another battalion was transporting him to us for treatment. The call came in over the radio at lunch time, when I was the only person still on duty. As soon as the ambulance pulled up I ran out with a bag of ice. My main concerns were for swelling, damage to his reproductive organs, and damage to his femoral artery. Reputedly the man had walked up to his "friends" who were on guard in a foxhole. One of these jokers lifted his M16 and fired at point blank range into the man's crotch. They said they didn't realize that blank rounds of ammunition could be dangerous. The blank had burned right through his BDU pants to his inner thigh and groin. He was embarrassed and in a great deal of pain. I ran over to our PA, who was eating his lunch, and asked if I could request a medevac for this patient. After getting the go ahead, I called in the request for a helicopter over the radio.

Unfortunately, I did not at all recall the proper 9 line format for calling in a medevac. I had learned it years ago and hadn't needed to use it since then. Now if we, as a medical unit, had practiced triage, medevac 9 lines, IVs, and treatment protocols all year long then things would have been different. Had our squad leaders spent part of our monthly drill rattling off mass casualty and traumatic injury scenarios, having us walk through the steps for treatment, and reciting the 9 line medevac call required, we would have been prepared for such an event. This was not the case and I tried to use a laminated 9 line card to help me walk through the call. For all I know I asked for an armed escort and two winches to pick-up three deceased soldiers that had been exposed to a biological agent, but were ambulatory and walking on their own. Yep, I probably called in the first ever 9 line medevac for zombies.

In the end, I hopped into the back of the ambulance and while the other two medics navigated their way over the uneven terrain to the LZ, I checked on the patient. All patients requiring an urgent evacuation had to arrive at the LZ with an IV line in place. Luckily, this incident occurred near the end of our two weeks in the woods, and by then starting IVs was old hat. While we bounced and bumped along, I braced myself to avoid falling, hung the IV bag, took a deep breath, and tore the cap off the catheter with my teeth. Then, very carefully, I inserted the needle into his arm and drained the air out of the IV tubing. This was no easy task, as the IV tubing was swinging around the back of that ambulance like one of those inflatable dancing tube men you might see outside of a carwash.

Although we were a bit queasy from the ride, we arrived safely at the LZ, popped a smoke canister to mark the site, and waited for the helicopter. The man was loaded aboard the Blackhawk helicopter and flown to a nearby hospital.

Since my mother and I were serving in the same battalion, we did cross one another's path during AT.

As someone who knew my mother's signature rather well, I could always spot a forged sick slip from someone from her company. I would look at the slip of paper and up at the soldier and ask, "Who signed this?" knowing their commander, my mother, had not.

One year my mother fractured her hand just before AT. She found it exceedingly inconvenient. It was difficult to open the doors on her Humvee, button up her BDU pants, or open her canteen for water. It was a particularly hot year and before too long my mom was visiting me with a case of dehydration and heat exhaustion. It had gotten to the point that she had passed out. Her condition was complicated by her uncooperative veins. She has really difficult veins for inserting an IV. They are small, they roll, and when she's dehydrated it's as if they magically disappear altogether. As a difficult case, her IV insertion was delegated up the chain to one of the platoon's physicians, a Lt Colonel. It didn't go well and my mom came to, swearing at the Lt Colonel. I don't think she's ever learned to take care of herself before taking care of other people.

It was nice to know someone with their own vehicle at camp. One evening I was walking to the laundry building with a huge sack of uniforms. My mom was driving past me and pulled over to give me a ride. I had to hop in the back seat, since one of her soldiers was sitting in the front. Humvees have really loud engines and I was straining to hear my mom's questions and comments. Then she suddenly swerved to the side of the road, turned around to face me and screamed at me, "Get out of the car! You know what to do!"

I had no idea what was going on, but you don't say no to my mother especially when she's screaming in your face. I got out of the vehicle and scanned the area. There was another HMMWV, a High Mobility Multipurpose Wheeled Vehicle, upside down in a sludge-filled ravine. Because the vehicle was hemmed in by the ravine, they couldn't get out through a door.

I crawled down towards the vehicle, opened the turret hatch, and slowly and carefully lowered each soldier out. Luckily, they hadn't sustained any major injuries and were really just shaking from nerves and adrenaline. They were able to place their hands on my shoulders as I unclipped their seat belts and lowered them through the turret.

After that, it was a stinky and messy matter of assisting them through the muck of decaying plant matter and up the steep hill to the road. There, I lined them up like ducks in a row and waited for the police.

I asked them what happened, and their stories didn't match

up. One said they didn't see the ravine. Another told the far more likely story. He said that they thought they could jump the ravine, or drive down and back up the incline. It turns out they in fact could not. When the first officer arrived on the scene, I asked him to have drug and alcohol testing done on the group.

This was the first of many occasions when my mother would pull over for an accident and yell at me to get out and do my thing. She's not one to ignore a situation, and I'm not either.

One year, a soldier wandered into my company's area of operation. He didn't know the password of the day, and couldn't say which company he was with or what he was doing in our area. My platoon immediately took him to be someone sent to test our security. They blindfolded him and carried him off to the dental treatment tent. There they tied him to the dental exam chair and threatened to do all manner of horrible things to him if he didn't tell them who he was and what he was doing there. I was unaware that this was going on. There were patients in the treatment area that I had to care for.

After they had run a dental drill next to his head, and threatened to use a defibrillator on him, he broke down crying. He finally was able to sob out that he didn't know what unit he was with but if we would call his commander, she would vouch for him. The only female commander at that time was my mother. My platoon got on the radio and before long my mother was there to collect her wayward soldier. One can only imagine how the verbal and emotional torture may have affected this poor young man.

There were other glaring issues with my company. One day, I watched as a surgical tech combed through a mound of surgical instruments he'd dumped on the floor of one of the bays in the supply area. As he attempted to inventory the jumbled pile of metal, he'd make offhand comments about what a mess everything was. There were rusty, dirty surgical instruments—some of which he said were meant to be used once and disposed of—intermixed with the rest. Can you imagine walking into a doctor's office and seeing someone sorting through a huge pile of dirty, rusty, and used medical instruments on the floor? Remembering that scene still gives me the creeps!

As part of our annual training, we had to "jump," moving our tent hospital from one spot in the woods to another. We had to pack up everything and transport all of the patients to a new site. Since this was not something we planned for or ever practiced, everything was always disorganized and disjointed. After one such jump, I had to use tweezers from someone's Swiss Army Knife to remove a tick from a general's ear. I did this because I could not locate the proper forceps. The saying, "there's a place for everything, and everything in its place," should be especially true in an Army Field Hospital. But for this unit, another saying, "Charlie Foxtrot," which actually stands for clusterfuck, was far more apropos. If instead we all worked together as a team, we would be optimizing the care of the men and women who trusted us with their lives.

18

JEAN: GET LOST

ANOTHER THING THAT ALWAYS FELT unsettling was the way men would act when they came to the treatment tent. Those who served in all-male units behaved as if they had never seen a woman before.

This was blatantly obvious in 1996, the year the summer Olympics were held in Atlanta, Georgia. The Army National Guard provided support and security for the event. As a result, a field infantry unit heading to Fort McCoy for annual training found itself two medics short. I had just completed AT at Fort McCoy when they asked for volunteers to support the incoming unit. My company wanted to supply them with two medics and an ambulance. I volunteered, as did Cali.

We reported to the unit's headquarters. I opened the door and stepped into a crowded office. All of the men looked at me, and then one said that he was glad that I was there, as they had a lot of typing that needed to be done. I'd never taken a typing class, and did not type. I gently informed them that I was there to provide emergency medical care for their personnel.

There were immediate challenges. No other women were in the unit, so I was housed alone in an empty barracks next door. My room had a lock, but the bathroom did not. I would walk into the bathroom and see men using the urinals there. This was supposed to be the "female" building.

Some of the large bathroom windows were painted over, but those that remained uncovered afforded a clear view inside the bathroom and shower area. Because anybody could just walk in—and they did—to take a shower I had to put a chair in front of the bathroom door and stay against the shower stall wall to shield myself from view. In many ways, I did not feel safe or in control.

In the barracks next door, the men had a frat house-type setup. At night, they played reel-to-reel pornographic films on a screen that someone had brought with them specifically for that purpose.

Cali was staying next door to me in the men's barracks. One night, he angrily insisted that we had to get married right away—that day, in fact. I don't know if someone said something to him about me or if he had heard some crude comments, but something had him rattled. I told him that I thought everything would be fine. We did not need to get married because of the antics of the men in his barracks. I could take care of myself, and we were only going to be there for two weeks, after all.

It wasn't as if he wanted to get married because he loved me desperately or thought an elopement would be romantic. I was confused and a little bit angry at Cali for acting like I was property to be marked, not someone who had been in an exclusive relationship with him for several years.

Things at Fort McCoy were tense and awkward, to my dismay and confusion. These men were only here for two weeks. Two weeks! The rest of the year, they held civilian jobs. They had to see women on a regular basis! They all had mothers and perhaps sisters, aunts, wives, daughters, and female civilian co-workers.

Still, why couldn't they adapt to having a female medic in their midst? Why did they giggle when they saw me? After a few days in the field, they had lost their minds.

After walking into the 'women's' bathroom and again catching a man using a urinal, I had had enough. It was my day off, so I walked to the base exchange phone booths to call my sister. I told her how all of the men were acting weird, how hard it was to take a shower, and how isolated and unsafe I felt. After venting a little, I felt better and walked back to the barracks. On the way there, I ran into Cali, and the two of us decided to hang out in my room until dinner.

What I didn't realize was that anything and everything I told my sister was immediately relayed to my mother. My mother, the Army Captain and Company Commander. My mother, who felt a bit overprotective of her daughters. Almost right after the call ended, my sister called our mom. If I had wanted my mom to know, I would have called her! I felt like I could deal with the situation for the remaining two weeks; I had just wanted to vent.

An hour or so later, we heard a sharp knock on my door. At that moment, Cali and I were naked, in bed. After quickly donning an oatmeal-colored linen maxi dress, barefoot and braless, I opened the door a crack. There stood a cadre of high-ranking officers. I felt all of the blood drain from my face. They informed me that they had spoken with my mom and were there to pack up my belongings and move me to the modern, safe, and distant base inn. I asked for a moment, and slammed and locked the door.

What was I to do?

Here was this group of officers ready to defend "a poor helpless female," and I had a naked man in my room! After a quick whispered argument, I pushed Cali into an empty wall locker, quickly changed into my uniform, and threw all of my belongings into a duffle bag. The officers and I headed out one side of the barracks, and as we did so I heard the far exit door slam closed. The noise frustrated me. Couldn't he have waited a few minutes? Couldn't he have been thoughtful and careful? Luckily, no one went to investigate the sound, but the incident added to my growing frustration with Cali.

The remainder of the two weeks was uneventful. Although I was embarrassed by the whole incident, and became far more cautious about what I said to my family members, I forgave and eventually appreciated my sister and mother's intervention.

After serving for four years with Charlie Company, I decided to apply for Officer Candidate School. I've always been outspoken, empathetic, and proactive. Being an officer seemed like a natural transition for me.

I took the Officer Selection Battery (OSB), gathered my letters of recommendation, and completed my OCS packet. At this same time, we learned that the battalion was going to be disbanded. We were all to be assigned to new units. Cali and I transferred to a new medical company with our OCS packets in hand. That weekend at drill, we handed over our packets and were told that the company commander would talk with us at the end of the day. Immediately, we realized that this unit was different. They were on the assembly floor doing skill testing. All of the tasks we had learned four years ago at AIT and had mostly forgotten were now back with a vengeance. At heart, I was excited to see all of the testing and activity. This was a unit that made things happen! They actually trained for the mission.

We joined the line of soldiers and went one at a time up to an evaluator and a casualty simulation dummy. There, the evaluator would list the signs and symptoms we'd find on a real patient. We were then to treat our fake plastic patient, see to fake blood and wounds, and answer any related questions from the evaluator. I was a good student during AIT and at the top of my class. I recalled enough to feel like I would get through the testing. Cali, however, was in a panic. He grabbed my arm and pulled me aside. Apparently, he did not feel confident and his "deer in the headlights" look startled me. I quickly ran through the steps to take in each scenario and reassured him. After all, a fail at any station meant that you'd receive a review of the task and retesting.

What I did not know was that this medical unit was about to be placed on Active Duty and sent to Bosnia. After lunch, the unit took inventory of all of their equipment. The doors were locked, and everyone was informed that they were shipping out. It seemed to take everyone by surprise. I was kind of excited, and told myself this was why I joined the military, to serve. This unit was what I had wanted to be a part of when I joined. They were driven, active, and trained to mission.

Cali and I, however, were called into the commander's office, and our OCS paperwork was sent forward. We were not going to be activated. We were not going to war. We were going to Springfield, Illinois.

OCS interested me, as it meant eighteen months of training, leadership lessons, and new friends and experiences. We started the first month with more than fifty or so other soldiers. Each month, that number dwindled. Individuals either asked to leave or simply gave up. The attrition rate was very high.

I excelled and was rated second in my class by my peers. Cali did not fare so well and felt he should have had a higher standing in the class. I tried to help my fellow candidates and printed little pocket-sized info sheets for everyone each month. I included the latest class roster, the monthly chain of command, tips, hints, and quick reference tools. I wanted everyone to do their best and make it through the program.

OCS was a big commitment. It meant extra physical and emotional strain. The majority of us were carrying a full course load at school. At the time, I was going to school, working full-time, and volunteering with a special recreation program. Committing to the OCS program meant driving three hours each way from our home in the Chicago suburbs to Camp Lincoln in Springfield, Illinois once a month. This was in addition to two weeks of training in Minneapolis and two weeks at Fort Benning, Georgia.

Both my mother and stepfather had taken a similar career path. They had both enlisted in the military, attended Officer Candidate School, and received their commissions in the U.S. Army.

After five years of spending two weeks each summer at annual training in a Wisconsin forest, I had learned that a menstrual period in the field is not great. You're not able to take daily showers; I think we were able to take one, if that. We were not on a schedule, and had no time off or to ourselves. If I got distracted, I might forget to change pads or tampons in a timely manner, risking infection and potentially toxic shock syndrome. I'd learned from past experience, and while in OCS, I took birth control without a break to avoid menstrual cycles and complications. By this time, I had also learned about menstrual cups, perfect for breakthrough bleeding.

When I learned that land navigation was part of OCS, I was not terribly concerned. It was a simple enough task: during daylight hours, and again at night, a TAC (training, advising, and counseling officer) would give each of us a list of grid coordinates. We would then draw out a route on a map to get to each point and set out to find the metal posts and signs for our assigned coordinates.

All we had to do was use a map, compass, protractor, pencil, and our know-how to locate our assigned points during the day and again at night, within a given time limit.

Of the 53,000 acres that encompass Camp Riley, Minnesota, only a small area of forest and open grassland is used for the land navigation course.

On the day of the test, I was excited! I love to be challenged and felt as if this was something I'd spent my life preparing to do.

As I broke through the tree line, on the top of a ridge I found a well-used gravel trail. A few feet from where I stood was a green metal post with a white sign. One point down! After writing the marker info on my test sheet, I crouched down on one knee to verify the compass direction for my next point.

Before I could set off for my second point, I heard someone nearby stepping on and snapping twigs as they broke through the tree line. I looked around. Well down the path, about halfway between my point and the next point on the ridge, I spotted someone I knew well. It was Cali!

He was out of breath and looked a bit wild around the eyes. It reminded me of the day of testing at our new and very temporary unit in Chicago. He looked scared and panicked. I was hesitant to speak with him. Our superiors had told us how important land navigation was. We were not to speak to anyone during the land navigation test unless there was a medical emergency. Doing so would be considered cheating and would result in automatic failure, dismissal from OCS, and possibly dishonorable discharge from the military. They took this seriously.

I had just about made up my mind to continue on, but then Cali ran up to me. He said that he could not complete the land navigation exam, that he did not know what he was doing, that he had not found any of his points, and that he was going to fail.

His words shocked me. I did not know what to do. I tried to reassure him. I told him that he could do it and not to give up. He insisted that he was unable to complete the test. To no avail, I told him not to worry and that everything would be OK.

As more people broke through the tree line and gathered around the point marker, he walked over to them and asked for help. I was shocked. We all knew we were not supposed to talk to one another, but there they were, talking. I walked away. I probably should have said something, at the time and later to my TAC officer, but I did not. I was in shock. This man I thought I had known for five years was not going to pass the test and was cheating. My future was suddenly uncertain.

The Uniform Code of Military Justice prohibits fraternization between enlisted soldiers and officers. *So,* I thought as I walked aimlessly off the trail and into the woods, *what now? If my future husband was not going to be able to continue, was not going to pass, and was not going to become an Army officer, how could I?* We'd been through so much together. I decided that I, too, would fail the land navigation practical exam. That evening during the nighttime portion of the land navigation exam, I intentionally looked for fireflies instead of my assigned points. I turned in my test paper with random answers. In my mind, I was doing what was best for our relationship. I was not really throwing in the towel, I was making it easier for Cali. He would not be alone. He wouldn't be the only one to fail. We'd still be together. Oh, I was such a total and complete fool.

Later that day, I was floored to learn that Cali had in fact passed the land navigation test, with a little help from his "friends." I felt betrayed, angry at myself and at Cali, and emotionally lost.

19

JEAN: A PATH DIVERGED

SINCE I HAD FAILED OUT of my OCS class, the 129th Training Regiment, which oversees training for the ILARNG, would have typically transferred me back to my previous unit in Chicago. However, the NCOs at the 129th Headquarters took the time to ask me what I intended to do in the future. After giving it a good deal of thought, I decided that I still wanted to be an officer with or without Cali. I wanted a second chance. I wanted to lead!

The 129th Regional Training Institute staff decided to allow me to become a temporary member of their staff until the next OCS class started. There was definitely a chasm forming between Cali and me. That winter, he flew home to California for the holidays alone. I stayed in Chicago. When he returned to Chicago in January, something about him had changed dramatically. Little courtesies, to which I'd become accustomed, were no longer observed.

For example, he would go to the kitchen to get himself something to drink, but he no longer asked if I would like anything. I felt a void opening up between us.

After a month of painful disquiet, he finally worked up the

nerve to tell me that he wanted to break off our engagement, and that he was planning on moving back to the West Coast.

I was crushed! We had our futures planned, and had worked so hard to be together. Now I was wrong-footed. Our split shouldn't have taken me by surprise. He was a serial dater who went from one relationship to the next. I found out we'd started dating while he had been seeing someone else. Apparently, he liked his relationships to overlap. We had been having problems with our relationship for some time and had never really worked them out. Whenever we disagreed about something, I always wanted to talk it out until we came to a resolution, while in contrast Cali quite literally ran away from confrontation. He packed up his tiny pick-up truck and drove back home.

Meanwhile, after a good deal of soul searching, I realized that I was far too empathetic to be in the medical field. Why was I pursuing a career for which I was so ill-suited? After a review of my academic strengths, I switched to a major in biochemistry and food science. I also began working full-time in an analytical chemistry laboratory for a petrochemical company.

It wasn't easy making the trek to Springfield every month by myself. It wasn't easy seeing Cali as he advanced through OCS and graduated without me. But I focused on what was coming next and set my sights on my future.

The following summer, I was back in the forest, and back on the land navigation course. This time I ran from point to point and felt assured that I was on the right path.

The next year at Fort Benning our attrition rate skyrocketed. Myself and many others got food poisoning. As if the heat and physical demands weren't enough, we were all vomiting or worse. Many candidates were so dehydrated that they lost consciousness and were taken to the hospital.

If you missed two or more days of training you were forced out of the program and had to start OCS over again. I was not about to start another rotation through OCS. Determined to stay conscious, I drank as much water as possible. As we ran from one area to the next, I would drop out of formation, vomit, and then catch back up. It was a sheer test of will and luck that got me through. The two things that surprised me the most were the swim test and water obstacle course.

After watching war movies, you may see the need for officers to be able to swim. If you are offloading on a beach, the ability to swim could save your life. To be honest, I thought the Senior OCS class was joking when they told us that there was a swim test. Not everyone knows how to swim. Wouldn't that have been something they asked about when you applied to OCS? Cali's mother, despite having been born on an island, has severe aquaphobia. I knew that there were those, like his mother, who would not even be able to get near the water.

One day we all went to an indoor pool. Those who did not swim received a basic introductory class before being asked to at least attempt the start of the water obstacle course. At the pool, one of the TAC officers said he would be teaching non-swimmers. He then proceeded to remove his BDU top, dive into the deep end with perfect form, and swim with long powerful strokes to the shallow end of the pool. It remains a very vivid image: as he stood up, the water at that end came up to his waist, giving us all a perfect view of his well defined torso. His brown t-shirt clung to his chest. At that point I think a number of us questioned whether or not we may need a nice refresher swimming course.

With more than a little regret at my ability to swim, I stayed at the deep end of the pool. For the first test we were attired in our standard field uniform, combat boots, and LBE (Load Bearing Equipment: a pistol belt, suspenders, two canteens, ammo pouches, and first aid bandage). We were then instructed to climb, one at a time, to the top of the high dive platform, where we would stand at the edge of the platform, blindfolded, and holding a rubber rifle out at arms length.

As I had volunteered to go first, and get it over with, I still thought: *this is a joke, right?* When I was all set, blindfold in place and faux weapon in hand, a TAC officer pushed me off the platform.

I learned how to swim before I learned how to read. So, although it was a bizarre situation, I could relatively easily drop into the deep end of the pool, surface, remove my blindfold, and swim to the edge.

After that, I had to swim the length of the pool while holding a rubber rifle out of the water. This was odd and challenging, but again I went first and accomplished the task. The only part of the testing that I had difficulty with involved wearing LBE, going under water, and holding your breath while you removed the pistol belt and gear. Unfortunately, the canteens on the test belt were empty and I kept bobbing to the surface like a cork. Once we remedied the situation, I was able to stay down long enough to remove the gear.

One of the other officer candidates pulled me aside after our day at the pool. She said when we first got to the pool she was terrified, for although she could swim, she had never jumped off a high dive before. But, she said she was reassured by the way I had volunteered to go first and made it all seem very easy.

That officer candidate had, to my surprise, failed land navigation the year before. When I found out, I went to speak with our commander. I told him that he had to give her another chance, because in my opinion with a simple refresher she would make an outstanding officer. She ended up retaking the test and passing.

Time flew by, and before I knew it I was receiving my commission and preparing for the next stage in my training, my Officer Basic Course (OBC).

After four months in the Chemical Officer Basic Course, or COBC, at Fort Leonard Wood, Missouri, I was second in my class. I would like to credit my academic prowess for my high class standing, but it was far more likely due to my ability to simply stay awake in my classes! At OBC the various physical, mental, and emotional demands made it difficult for many people to stay awake at their desks.

But I had a strategy. I went to bed early, woke up early, and did yoga and Pilates in my studio apartment before heading to PT. To get through the long days of classes, I drank cup after cup of iced espresso without cream or sugar, and chewed caffeinated gum. I was one-part military officer and two parts straight caffeine. I also ate a healthy diet, full of lean protein and vegetables, and abstained from alcohol during the week.

At the end of the workday, I would go for a run and take kickboxing classes at the on-post gym. I was driven to succeed and looked forward to a long military career. At the time, I was financially stable. I had savings, stocks, CDs, and a new car. Back home, I was living next door to my parents, in my deceased step-grandmother's old home, for which she had paid in cash. In addition to a great civilian job, I had already served seven years in the military.

At that time, I was occasionally seeing a brilliant older man, James, who was taking classes at the Army War College.

We had initially met in 1995 or 1996, during our Illinois Army National Guard Battalion's Annual Training in Wisconsin. I was an enlisted combat medic/EMT. Another medic and I sat in a Humvee ambulance and provided coverage for a unit qualifying at one of the Fort McCoy shooting ranges. If someone was shot or otherwise injured, we were there to provide emergency medical care and transport them to the nearest hospital.

It was a hot summer, and thankfully an uneventful day. At one point, James, a Major with the ILARNG at that time, stopped by the ambulance and started asking questions. He wanted to know how we would treat patients in the event of a Nuclear, Biological, or Chemical (NBC) attack. I looked at the emblem on his collar, two retort flasks crossed over a benzene ring, and realized the reason for his line of questioning. He was part of the Chemical Corp. I racked my brain for the little we were told about treating and transporting patients in such circumstances at AIT at Fort Sam Houston. C Company had never discussed or trained to treat or transport NBC casualties. We didn't even have the VBS-93 casualty bags, which look like body bags with a clear viewing window and ventilation port. I never learned how to hook such equipment up to the ambulance's air filtration and ventilation system, or even knew how to turn the system on for that matter. We would come across faux NBC casualties during a mass casualty exercise one annual training. Unfortunately, even then, we did not learn or practice the proper NBC procedures. We only discussed them briefly during our after-action review.

While talking with James, the Major, I did my best to describe what I could recall from Ft. Sam and answered his insightful questions. After the unit was finished at the shooting range, I packed up the ambulance and returned to my unit's area of operations. Our Annual Training ended, and I returned to my civilian job and college classes.

In 1998, I was working at my civilian job in the analytical laboratory of a petrochemical company, in McCook, Illinois. I would work from four in the afternoon till midnight. This allowed me to help watch my sister's three boys during the day and continue taking college classes. By six at night, the lab was dead quiet. I had three labs all to myself. On the plus side, I could run a number of experiments at the same time and work at my own pace. On the downside, around ten at night, I was often bored and tired of the isolation.

This was a time before smartphones, apps, and streaming music. To keep myself awake, and feel connected, I would log on to online chat rooms and chat with friends and strangers.

I'd been separated from Cali for some time, and was back in the dating arena. I wanted to feel like I was still desirable and dateable, as at the time I really felt broken and fragile. After chatting with a number of men online and on the phone, I decided to meet a few of them in real life. Although I had hoped to meet someone who had their life together and knew who they were and what they wanted, money and financial status were not real concerns for me.

One suitor was a telephone repair guy. We decided to meet at his place to watch the Super Bowl on TV. For some reason, I thought this would be a group activity. I had pictured a Super Bowl party in my mind, but it was just the two of us. He had made snack foods for us to eat, but the fact that there was no hand soap or hand towels in his bathroom took away my appetite. How could he cook without washing his hands? A wet bath towel and mattress on the floor, the lack of soap anywhere to be seen, and his odd vibe were all too much for me. After the football game, he asked if I would go with him to drop off some keys. I obliged, and soon realized that we were going to meet his ex-wife. Apparently, I was a prop, the "I'm over you and dating someone else already" gal. I did not see him again.

Then there was the UIC student. He was sweet and used his student ID to get discounts everywhere. Apparently, he had either never kissed anyone before, or no one had ever told him that you're not really supposed to try and eat someone's face when you kiss. There was way too much saliva, tongue, teeth, and sucking action. At one point I thought I was being vacuumed up, or that I might drown while kissing him. He was too new and shiny for me.

I also briefly dated a young man who lived in Springfield Illinois, about three and a half hours from my home. I drove down to Springfield once a month for OCS, so we only saw one another briefly, and our interactions were always a bit odd. He would hang out with me the Friday before OCS, and always asked if he could try on my Army uniform. We never really clicked.

I wanted to date someone who had some experience dating,

washed his hands after he went to the bathroom, and with whom I had shared interests and experiences.

I started chatting online with a fellow member of the ILARNG, James. He was witty, and his range of knowledge was extremely diverse. After a few weeks of conversation, we decided to meet in person.

He made reservations at a restaurant downtown, and I was shocked when I walked up to the table and saw that the man I had been corresponding with was the same chemical officer I had met years before at Fort McCoy in Wisconsin. People often say it's a small world, and on this occasion I had to agree. We had a wonderful meal, walked through the busy streets of Chicago, and even took a horse-drawn carriage ride. His wit and wisdom made me swoon.

On that first date, James did say something that put me on my back foot, and made me question whether or not he felt that we were well suited to date. At the end of the evening, he said something along the lines of, "What would you have thought if I'd shown up for our date dressed like you?"

I was wearing the typical little black dress, heels, and scarf for a splash of color. It was a bit chilly, and I hadn't worn a coat that evening. I thought he meant that I was dressed inappropriately, and was making fun of me. In reality, he was talking about dressing exactly the way I was, dress, heels, and all. I was very naïve, and never even considered that he had meant his words literally.

At that time, 1998, James was thinking about hiring a librarian to organize his collection of military books, his boys were quite young, and his daughter was taking ballet lessons. He was also planning a scientific expedition to the Antarctic to collect meteorites. He was a gallant and utterly fascinating man, and I was thrilled to have met someone who knew what he wanted in life.

James and I saw one another a few more times before I headed to Fort Leonard Wood and OBC in the Fall of 1999. We even had a chance to take my nephews to the Shedd Aquarium and the Adler Planetarium.

This Shedd trip was another outing that made me question if James even liked me a little. We had taken my nephews, Sean and Devin, to the aquarium. It was snowing and very cold. He walked us back to my car, and it would not start. I was at a loss as to what to do next. The car was parked on East Solidarity Drive, closer to the Adler Planetarium than the Shedd Aquarium. So, James suggested that we walk over to the Planetarium, call for a tow truck, and stay warm. We all walked over, and as I called my mom to come and pick us up, we grabbed lunch and a seat in the Cafe Galileo.

As we sat there eating, an older couple came over to our table. They greeted James, who stood up to exchange pleasantries, and then turned towards me as if inviting an introduction. James glanced over his shoulder at me and then turned back to the couple and said something that I perceived as dismissive and distancing, along the lines of "Oh, her car broke down." No exchange of names or introductions. With that, the couple left, and I sat there feeling a little deflated.

When I headed out of state for my stint at OBC in Missouri, I wasn't entirely sure where James and I stood. I left having convinced myself that he thought I didn't know how to dress and wasn't important enough to introduce to people he knew. I thought *okay, so this is an amazing, intelligent man who's not really interested in me.* It felt like another denial. I thought we'd wait and see how things went and see how we both felt when I got back. I think this sense of rejection, based on misconceptions, heightened my weird emotional state at that time.

OBC was to be a quick stop on the road to my future. Although I was physically fit and doing well in class, I was an emotional wreck. I was angry, frustrated, and unhappy.

People arrived at OBC from five different paths. There were

a handful of individuals who, like me, had enlisted in the Army, went through basic training and AIT, spent time in the enlisted ranks, and were selected for OCS. We knew what it was like to be a soldier. Then there were two enlisted soldiers in my OBC who had served for many years, were too old for OCS, and had received a direct commission instead. Our class did not have any military academy or West Point graduates, but that's another way to obtain a commission. We had one officer in our class from Bahrain. The largest contingent of officers in my class were from ROTC (Reserve Officers' Training Corps). They were recent college graduates with no experience in the enlisted ranks.

I was often embarrassed by the antics of some of the ROTC grads. At one point during field training, we were followed by a film crew while we filled sandbags and moved them to form a mound in front of foxhole fighting positions. Two female ROTC officers were acting like fools. They giggled, bumbled the sandbags, and tripped over their own feet. Bile rose in my throat as I watched these two bring shame to women and officers everywhere, and on film no less. They would be immortalized as buffoons by the media crew.

When you are in uniform, you represent all members of that service. You have to act above reproach. You don't slouch. You don't put your hands in your pockets. You never lean against a wall or anything else for that matter. You walk tall, proud, and with your emotions repressed. I was never very good at that last one. I still cry, even though my mother tried to train that out of me.

My mother taught me that as a woman in the military, you needed to be strong and confident, and push yourself. These two female officers were acting weak, silly, and clumsy. They were an embarrassment to female soldiers everywhere. We were supposed to be officers, set the example, and be above reproach. These were the same two who said that they had "deep throated" fellow classmates during their microbiology finals.

This apparently meant that they had swabbed their own throats. Then they took that mixture of biological material and smeared the swab across the agar plates of fellow classmates. This would make it impossible for their classmates to pass the practical and meant that they had possibly failed the class.

Their lack of morals and empathy made me dislike them even more. It was shocking to me to meet someone who would go out of their way to ensure that others failed. It made me sick to think that they were officers and would be responsible for the lives and welfare of soldiers.

One of these terrible twosome even started dating an enlisted trainee on base, which was something verboten by the Uniform Code of Military Justice, and something I saw as deeply inappropriate.

Although the involved parties were not in the same chain of command, as Army Regulation AR600-2, Section 4-14b emphasized, in this kind of relationship the integrity of supervisory authority was at risk and potential for coercive and unfair, predatory behavior was more than present.

I often witnessed, to my horror, the enlisted soldier sneaking out at the break of dawn.

She even tried setting me up with his friend.

I told her, "No, it's against the regulations, and I'm seeing someone at home."

This was not some excuse. This was true, and I was thrilled to be able to say as much.

In February, I received a Valentine's Day package from James containing two wonderful academic books about the Chemical Corps that gave me new insight into the cooperation of allied nations in research and development. This gift was really meaningful to me, as it underlined how this was a thoughtful and committed relationship.

In March, I went with a group of five of my fellow OBC

classmates to New Orleans for a long weekend. We drove down in my car and stayed with one of my classmates' friends, a medical student at Tulane. I'd never been to New Orleans before. I was surprised by the fact that you could purchase drinks at any of the drive-thru bars. I was enchanted by the architecture, the small antique and custom jewelry shops, and Spanish moss dripping cypress. It was a very brief but interesting break from classes, and a chance to relax.

Later that month, my platoon decided to participate in an extracurricular activity. One of my classmates coordinated with a member of the German Armed Forces to provide extra training and the chance to earn the German Armed Forces Proficiency Badge (GAFPB). The GAFPB is a decoration of the Bundeswehr, the Armed Forces of the Federal Republic of Germany, one of several awards that Allied soldiers can earn. In the United States military, the GAFPB, a large medal of an eagle, is one of the few approved foreign awards that may be worn on the dress uniform. It is also one of the most sought-after awards to achieve. I wanted the added challenge. I wanted to prove myself worthy. I wanted to do something I could look back on and be proud of.

There were three possible medals to earn, a bronze, silver, or gold eagle. I knew if I earned the gold eagle, I would prove myself to my peers. I would hold my chest even higher while in formation with the gleaming gold eagle above my name plate.

This badge is solely based on physical proficiency. It is laid out in a type of extreme decathlon. In a combination of track and field, weapon qualification, and other events, an applicant would test their endurance. One had to swim 100 meters, qualify with a double-action Glock, finish a timed fifteen-mile road march with full pack and an M16 weapon, conduct a sprint run of 11 x 10 meters, perform a high jump, and offer other displays of physical prowess.

The high jump was the final event in the series, and I had

successfully completed each of the other events. Unfortunately, I had never seen a high jump prior to that day.

Being unaccustomed to the event, I ran up to the bar, stopped before reaching it, and propelled myself upward and in a duck and roll over it, head first with my back parallel to the ground as I rolled. I landed hard on my head, neck, back, and left shoulder.

The impact with the mat was hard, and left me unconscious for a moment. Then, excruciating waves of pain surging through my head, neck, shoulder, and upper back—more pain than I had ever felt before—took my breath away. As I landed, I knew that there was something wrong, because when I became aware of my surroundings I heard gasps. But I wasn't done yet. It turned out that my foot had touched the bar and knocked it off the standards holding it in place, disqualifying my attempt. I was allowed another attempt.

The pain had started to subside, although my ears were ringing and my head throbbing. I returned to the starting point, asked what I did wrong, and tried to put "lift your legs" in my mind as I ran toward the bar one last time.

The second attempt was successful in terms of the competition. I had just placed myself squarely in position to receive the highest level of GAFPB, the gold medal. The second impact was hard enough to knock me out, which may have been a blessing. The pain might have been even worse the second time around. When I came to, my head was pounding, my eyes wouldn't focus, my ears were still ringing, and my neck and shoulder felt like they had been ripped off of my body.

I thought I would be OK. After all, we were often told that pain was just weakness leaving the body. But in this case, unbeknownst to me, the pain was from a traumatic brain injury, my brain squeezing through the base of my skull, compressing my spinal cord and cerebellum, muscles tearing off my left shoulder blade, my skull dropping closer to my torso from torn ligaments, tendons, and muscles in my neck, and other smaller injuries. It wasn't until the next morning that I went to the ER.

In the hospital, I held back the scream that rose in my throat and was quickly quelled with an IV sedative. I spent the rest of the day hospitalized, in traction. The pain meds that were injected into my veins made me queasy, but put me in a pain-free state of solid sleep.

If my unit, or the German unit that was conducting the event, had followed any typical safety requirements, there probably would have been a better outcome. Unfortunately, high jump mats were not used. Instead, tumbling mats were piled on top of each other. The total height may or may not have reached the required minimum of twenty inches. However, due to the nature of a tumbling mat (hard, thin, and noncompressible) simply layering one on top of another did not provide the required energy displacement as my upper body made contact with the mat after being thrust up and over a horizontal pole. The landing was not as cushioned as it should have been, and caused my injury.

The next day, I awoke to my mother and stepfather sitting near my bed with worried looks on their faces. I stirred quickly, and said, "I think I made the gold!"

20

JEAN: NOT ALL INJURIES COME IN COMBAT

MY PARENTS WERE CONCERNED ABOUT possible long-term effects. Knowing more than I did about how the military system works, they immediately asked about my Line of Duty (LOD) form. Injuries, illness, disabilities, and deaths are either deemed in the Line of Duty or not. If your injury is determined not to be in the LOD, then you may be footing the bill for all medical care. The doctor who was releasing me didn't have a copy of my LOD, and didn't know if one had been started.

The very next stop: my unit headquarters. My company commander was not to be found. He was in the dentist's office, and was going on medical leave from there. The executive officer was nowhere to be found either, and the first sergeant was also gone. The office was essentially vacant while everyone was getting ready for graduation the next day.

Graduation! I needed to get ready for graduation!

My folks would not listen. Their next stop: a step up the chain of command to the battalion sergeant major's office. After a brief introduction, the sergeant major said he absolutely appreciated our concern and would track down the Executive Officer (XO) to get the LOD rolling. By the end of the day, my LOD was delivered to me at my Bachelor Officer Quarters (BOQ).

While we were waiting, my parents packed up all of my gear and made sure my uniform was ready for the graduation ceremony the following day. Cars packed up, we turned in the keys for the BOQ and retreated to the hotel where my parents had two adjoining rooms booked. One room was for my mom and me, so she could watch over me, and the other was for my stepdad.

The next morning, after the three of us donned our uniforms, we made our way to the hall where graduation services would take place. I was still in a neck collar and felt out of place. I don't recall a great deal of the ceremony, outprocessing, or anything else from this time. Everything felt like it was moving too fast. I was taking very strong prescription muscle relaxants and pain medication, which knocked me out.

My parents drove my car, all of my belongings, and me back home to Illinois. They put my things in their basement, which promptly flooded. Six feet of sewage and water filled the basement up to the rafters. I lost nearly everything: clothes, furniture, paperwork, and books.

But life went on, and I still had to report to my new National Guard unit back in Illinois, a chemical company in Machesney Park, near Rockford, an hour and a half drive from my home. My mother drove me out a few days after we arrived home and weeks prior to drill weekend, with the LOD.

We asked the unit administrator, an E-6, which medical facility would be following up on my care. We were told we would hear back in a day or so. The unit commander called a few days later, and insisted that I report to duty for drill; this was two weeks after my return from graduating Officer Basic and being injured and not yet treated at a medical facility.

My mother was livid. My drill weekend was the same as hers.

She was now in the Army Reserves at the Eighty-Fifth Division in Arlington Heights. She spoke with her full-time counterpart, an Army Lieutenant Colonel whom she and my stepfather both knew from competitive pistol shooting outside of the Guard. He told her to do what she had to do. He could hold down the office duties in her absence.

My mom drove me out to drill, and we were the first to arrive at 0530. I think she had hoped we could talk sense into my company commander, and I would be put on profile, meaning that I would be excused from further drill meetings until I was fully healed. We also had to find out about medical care since no one had gotten back to me yet in that regard.

The meeting with my Commanding Officer (CO) went as I would have expected. He had no clue as to where I should go for my injury. This wasn't something he had had to deal with before, and no one knew what to do with me. Finally, the state set up an appointment for me at Ft. Knox to finalize my LOD.

I flew to Fort Knox, about 330 miles from my home, and saw a physician's assistant. She said I had a strain in my cervical spine and would be just fine in a few weeks.

I was then sent to the hospital at Great Lakes Naval Base. They said I lived too far away to be treated there. So, my unit made arrangements with the ILARNG command in Springfield and I was able to have physical therapy at a hospital near my home, Loyola University Medical Center.

My commander insisted that I still attend monthly drill weekends. I was taking prescription muscle relaxants and pain medication and was unable to drive. An acquaintance OCS, Lieutenant Susan Kemnetz, and my mother took turns driving me to drill weekends.

I wasn't recovering. In fact, I was getting much worse. At first, I had constant headaches, nausea, and dizziness, which I thought was temporary, but they never went away. My eyes did not always move together and one would look off to the side when I wanted to look straight ahead. The pupils of my eyes were no longer the same size and no longer reacted equally when the light changed. If it was just a simple strain, then why did my eyes jerk and stutter when I tried to watch television? I thought I was losing my mind. My sense of smell was so heightened that I got queasy whenever anyone cooked meat and had to stay out of the kitchen. I had no gag reflex, and was constantly choking on food and water. My left arm was getting weaker and weaker by the day, despite PT. I kept dropping things, and we soon had to switch out our glassware and china for plastic and paper.

I was blacking out or fainting every time I changed position. I would try to stand up from a chair and would find myself on the floor, I fell going both up and down stairs. My left hand would cramp into a ball and had to be massaged flat. My ring finger and pinky on my left hand remained at a weird bent angle and would not straighten out.

My blood pressure would bottom out without warning and I would lose consciousness and stop breathing, especially at night. Neither my digestive or urinary systems were working properly.

My ability to communicate was affected as well. I felt like I was in a shell, and couldn't break through and express my thoughts. Enough cannot be said about the pain I have experienced as a result of my injuries—throbbing, stabbing, burning, tearing, gnawing, constant, and intermittent pain. I found that pain medicine either knocked me out or dulled my senses. Nothing has ever stopped the pain.

I was still trying to work, go to school, and date. My lab hired a college student who was studying chemistry to help me, but it wasn't enough. I had great difficulty reaching into the glove box to run experiments and I would drop samples on the ground, smashing the glass containers and displacing the contents. When working with platinum, mercury, jet fuel, and other expensive, toxic, or highly flammable chemicals, accidents can be a big problem. After a while, I was out of work. School was also a challenge. I couldn't focus and had difficulty finding the right words, so that was put on hold as well. I stopped dating and talking to friends, and withdrew from life.

Logistics were rough, since there was little communication between my new unit and Fort Knox. Several appointments I had were canceled while I was en route. I only found out they wouldn't take place when I arrived at the medical sites.

One day, I received a letter in the mail stating that I was to report to the Fort Knox VA that very afternoon for an MRI. Fort Knox was a five-hour drive from my home. There was no way I could get there in time. I contacted my unit, they made airline reservations for me for a future date, and said that they had rescheduled my appointment.

Traveling was very painful for me. I couldn't get comfortable, was always afraid I would fall or faint at the airport, and couldn't eat or drink anything in case I choked. Whoever accompanied me, typically my mother or great-aunt Mary, would have to pay for their own ticket.

When I arrived at the Ft. Knox VA the following Saturday for my MRI, they had no record of any appointment and didn't know who I was or why I was there. It was a weekend, and there was no one at my unit, no one at state, and nothing to do but sit in the lobby of the VA hospital while a flash flood washed out the exit road.

When I finally got back to Chicago, my mother was furious. She saw how hard traveling was for me. She couldn't believe that I had to fly out of state for an MRI when there were plenty of hospitals and MRI facilities near my home. She was angry that someone had dropped the ball and no appointment had been made. She was upset because we had gone to all that trouble for nothing. I was in an extraordinary amount of pain and discomfort.

I wanted answers, but found nothing but frustration.

In the end, I had an MRI of my C-spine at Loyola and they said it looked fine. It wasn't fine. Years later, when we requested a copy of the MRI report from Loyola, I believe it had been changed. Based on my memory of the original, it appeared someone had gone in and rewritten the report. Now it clearly outlined the extent of my injuries.

In the meantime, Loyola stopped accepting my insurance, and I was left in limbo without care. After repeated requests to my unit, state, and Congress, I was assigned to Great Lakes Naval Base for treatment until I could be discharged. The distance from my home had not changed, but that didn't seem to matter. I started going to Great Lakes for physical therapy and physical exams.

Because I lived so far away, they tried to schedule all of my appointments on the same day. I would go from office to office, seeing the orthopedist, neurologist, physiatrist, and a physician from the pain clinic.

I was taking prescription pain medicine during this entire time. I was prescribed nonsteroidal anti-inflammatories, Celebrex, meloxicam, topical capsaicin, Flexeril, Baclofen, gabapentin, nortriptyline, Vicodin, Valium, and many other medications. Then there were the opiods: hydrocodone, fentanyl, methadone, codeine, morphine, and oxycodone. The orthopedist would tell me that my neck injury was causing my shoulder, arm, and hand pain. At my next appointment, ten minutes later and across the hall, the next physician would inform me that my pain and weakness was all from my shoulder injury.

At one point, my mom, who was with me said, "Why don't they open the doors and meet in the hall and TALK TOGETHER!"

But Great Lakes was where I was going for treatment, not diagnosis. They were only able to carry out the orders for treatment supplied by the PA from Ft. Knox.

The doctors prescribed me three more months of physical

therapy and more pain medicine, and we left for home once again. Fort Knox began Medical Discharge Board proceedings, creating a paper exam of my medical files.

Based on this review, I was placed on TDRL, the Temporary Disability Retirement List. This gave the doctors up to eighteen months, I believe, to "fix" me before I was boarded out and would receive some type of medical discharge. If I was given a medical discharge for a simple cervical strain, I would not receive retirement, VA medical care, or any further medical treatment from them.

This time, when I called my commander with an update, I was informed that I was being transferred to a unit in Chicago. They felt this new unit would be able to handle my admin issues.

My mom and I felt this was a really smart move. I was ordered to report to my new commander. We went downtown on the appointed day, at the appointed time, but no one was there. It was like the Ft. Knox VA all over again. It felt like they were making things hard on me for no reason. Getting ready for this ordered appointment was hard. I had to take a shower while my mom sat in the bathroom in case I blacked out. Showering was painful, as my lack of balance and coordination and the lack of range of motion on my left side made it very difficult. The only shirts I could put on were button down shirts because I couldn't lift my left arm up, out, or back. Sitting in a car in rush hour traffic, in pain, while trying not to vomit, was terrible. When no one was there to meet us, it felt like an affront.

My commander was surprisingly very angry with me! He said that I should have waited. This incident pushed me into a deep depression. I felt that I was already suffering, and now I was facing the ire of the ILARNG. My mom was pissed, and after a call to our Congressman, the unit assigned a Captain to oversee my case and make home visits.

This wasn't any old person, this was the now Captain "Lemon," the same bitter little man who oversaw my mother's Report of Survey when she left company command. Because of his lack of due diligence, my mother almost ended up in jail. Needless to say, he was not welcome in our home. We soon noticed derogatory comments about my mother and me in the documentation Lemon sent to the state. In memorandums for record he referred to my mom as "that interfering woman."

It truly harms a soldier to feel that they do not have the support of their command. Lemon treated me with disrespect. His utter lack of empathy and disdain were a sad testament to his inability to lead. How can you constantly berate a fellow officer, let alone one who has been severely injured on active duty?

He blamed me for the long delays in obtaining medical documentation from hospitals. I do not now, nor have I ever, had any sway over the records departments or the stringent policies they put in place to safeguard personal medical information.

I'm still angry. I would receive a memorandum informing me that if I failed to supply whatever requested documentation, I would be discharged from the service. I would receive such letters via certified mail, post-dated after the due date, for me to accomplish these impossible tasks.

Yet when my "command" failed to set up an appointment, for which I had packed a bag, waited at an airport, flown out of state, checked into a hotel, and arrived in agony, they didn't even have the decency to apologize. My command wanted me to show up for drill weekends, as if I was not struggling to simply get out of bed. But somehow I persevered. I tried to keep all of my correspondence aboveboard and professional.

It was hard to show up for appointments, often out of state, only to find out that there was no appointment. Then my superiors would inform me that I was not to cancel my appointments and would be violating a direct order if I did not make it to all of my appointments. I never cancelled an appointment. I would arrive for an appointment and check in, and the medical staff would look at me in confusion. Did someone forget to make the appointment for me? Did they cancel it on purpose? I have no idea what was going on. Most of my out of state appointments, which could just as easily have been scheduled locally, required that I fly out the day before, stay overnight, and then fly back home. Did they really think I would go to all of the trouble to sit in an airport, suffer through a bumpy flight, sleep in a strange bed, and then cancel or not show up for an appointment?

I was berated for not sending Lemon copies of my medical records. I sent out reams of medical files. Someone told me later that Lemon had drawers full of my confidential medical information. Shouldn't he have been forwarding my paperwork to the state? Shouldn't someone have overseen his work and ensured that my privacy was respected?

With the negative, unsupportive, abusive, and cruel haranguing from my command, my depression started to overwhelm me as my physical condition deteriorated further. I was spending more and more time in bed, and withdrew further from friends and family.

When the physicians treating me at Great Lakes found out that I was going to be discharged for a cervical strain, they were extremely concerned. Again, I was treated with physical therapy for months, but no improvement was made until they brought in a specialist at the Great Lakes Naval Hospital.

During the neuro exam, I did everything I had done on numerous other occasions—testing the strength in my arms, my balance, and my ability to grip a pencil with each hand, all while comparing my right side to my left.

My left hand and arm ought to have been strongest, since I am left-handed, but now it was clearly my weaker side. Then the doctor had me perform a grimace with my teeth, pushing my jaw forward, tightening my neck muscles as I did so. While grimacing, the muscles in your neck tighten. For me, the left side was slack. The muscles in my face and neck had atrophied. The doctor called a neurosurgeon into the room and said, "It's not her neck. It's her brain!" The muscles on one side of my face, neck, shoulder, arm, and hand were wasting away. They requested that my medical discharge board be placed on hold while they took a closer look at my condition. They requested a full series of MRIs and then sat me down to inform me that I needed surgery. The results were shocking.

The physician told me that my tonsils had herniated out of my skull. *Well, my tonsils had been removed years before, so how could they have herniated out of my skull? What were they doing IN my skull? Shouldn't they be in my throat? That is, if I hadn't already had them removed?*

As it turns out, they were referring to cerebral tonsils, which are two small pieces of brain sitting at the lowest part of the skull at the back of your head. Mine were no longer in place. Instead, they had squeezed through the opening of the bony skull at the bottom where your spinal cord starts. They were putting pressure on my brain stem and reducing the flow of cerebrospinal fluid.

Because you have to have a stable medical condition before you can receive a medical discharge, I would have to have brain surgery.

21
JEAN: SOME BONES TO PICK

BY THIS TIME, FOUR YEARS had passed since my injury, and the United States was at war in Iraq. Fort Knox did not have a neurosurgeon on staff. Most of the Army surgeons were now stationed overseas to treat soldiers injured in combat. I would have to wait for a rotating specialist to make their rounds from one of the other military bases within the Great Lakes region.

Several months later, I was scheduled to meet with a surgeon. We drove down to Fort Knox, and I was surprised to find that my mom had booked us a room at the Newgarden Inn. This lodging is not to be missed if you ever get a chance to visit!

The room was a bedroom suite with a full living room and kitchen. Antique early American Federalist furniture filled it, and beautiful pictures of previous fort commanders lined the halls. We were the only soldiers in the building. I think they were just happy to have paying customers.

The visiting doctor recommended that we go to Wright-Patterson Air Force Base in Ohio, another super long drive away! The neurosurgeon at Wright was the only doctor he knew of who had any knowledge in this type of procedure. We were scheduled to see this new neurosurgeon the following month.

My mom accompanied me to my appointment there. The doctor introduced himself and explained that he had reviewed the chart and MRIs, and could do the surgery whenever we wanted.

He then explained what the surgery would entail: a craniectomy, laminectomy, and decompression, with possible shunts. Basically he would be removing the back part of my skull to allow the brain tissue more space to possibly retract back up into the area it belonged in and then securing the area with a bovine dura tissue patch. I should be good to go in no time!

Then, however, my mom asked a question I never would have thought to ask: "What is your personal success rate with this particular surgery?"

The doctor's face turned beet red as he confessed, "Well, I have never actually done the procedure myself, but I did observe one during my residency."

Nothing else needed to be said. I could see that my mother was not handling this news with a cool head. After a few minutes of silence, in which I thought the next world war might be brewing in this very room, she said, "Would you want someone operating on *your* daughter if they had no previous experience?" He said he understood, and with that, we left. The drive home might have been a bit faster than the ride down.

My mom then went on a quest to find a qualified neurosurgeon. A pediatric neurosurgeon at the University of Chicago performed the required procedure several times a day. He was overqualified. We wrote to Congress and requested that I receive care from a qualified physician outside of the normal military channels. After months of back and forth, the doctor agreed to perform the procedure, and my surgery was scheduled. It was not an easy thing to recover from.

Unfortunately, a year later, the pain in my shoulder blade was still there, and my arm and hand were weaker yet. I returned to the University of Chicago, and saw an orthopedic surgeon.

The surgeon said that the problem was obvious and that he could perform a surgical repair. He did caution me that the rehab and recovery would be long and painful. Since I had already tolerated this pain for several years by now, I jumped at the opportunity, and was scheduled for surgery.

During the procedure, my scapula was lifted away from my rib cage, and a section of the bone was removed.

After brain and shoulder surgery, I felt useless. Worse than useless, I was a drain. I needed help with everything. Someone helped me bathe, eat, dress, and get in and out of bed. I say bed, but I was sleeping in a lift chair. From the time I woke up in the morning until I went to bed at night, I needed assistance. My depression grew with each day. I felt as if I had lost everything. I no longer had a home of my own, privacy, a career, or a future. I didn't want to impose on my family, limit their activities, or be a burden.

One day, when I was feeling especially low, I received a call from the National Bone Marrow Registry. Years before, I had added my cheek swab to the millions of others who wanted to help those who need a bone marrow donation. I've always felt strongly about helping others, and regularly donated blood and platelets. They were calling to inform me that I was a match. At a point in my life when I felt that I no longer served a purpose, here this organization was asking if I was still interested in saving a life. My immediate reaction: "Hell yes!"

I received a packet from the registry in the mail. It was a detailed questionnaire to update my health information and begin the donation process. On a page of disqualifying medical conditions, including leprosy, cancer, and AIDS, was brain surgery with a bovine dura matter patch. I called right away and learned that I was no longer eligible to donate bone marrow, blood, or other tissue. Needless to say, that broke my heart.

My sister, who by this time had three children and was recently divorced, moved into the house next door. When she heard about the bone marrow kerfuffle, she immediately said she would donate in my place. But she was also disqualified because of a previous bone graft.

It was wonderful having my sister and her boys right next door. We could have family dinners on a daily basis. A year or so later, I woke early one morning to a loud banging on the front door. There stood my sister, tears streaming down her face, her three boys still in their pajamas, clutching her. In a panicked voice, she told us that her house was on fire.

The fire gutted the house, leaving a gaping hole in the dining room floor that opened up to the basement below. They lost everything, including two pets. To this day, nearly twenty years later, my sister still has the melted plastic smoke detector that woke her up that morning, saving her life and those of her children.

It took months to clean, repair, and rebuild the house. In the end, my sister realized that she couldn't live there anymore. Despite everything being shiny and new, she insisted that she smelled phantom smoke in every room. So she found a new home, and she and her children moved to Lockport, Illinois. It was very hard to go from seeing my nephews every day to seeing them a few times a month.

The National Guard considered me stable and ready for discharge after my shoulder procedure. Because of the war and all of the new Line of Duty injuries and medical discharges, there was a backlog and my file was placed at the bottom of the pile. Ft. Knox informed me that I would no longer need to fly to Kentucky for evaluation, and that I could see an assigned physician in Chicago for my final evaluation prior to my discharge board.

The physician whom they assigned me to see was not an orthopedist or neurologist. He did a lot of testifying in court. The impression I got was that he worked the facts around and tailored his diagnoses to order. No matter what had happened to a patient, he would come up with the conclusion that the injured party was at fault, born that way, or just faking it. The appointment was very odd. Before he even examined me, he stated that my injuries were because my legs were of different lengths. I had never heard that before. My hips were aligned, and my legs did not look as if they were any different. Besides, I was fairly sure that my injuries were actually caused by my impact with a hard surface, not the length of my legs.

By this time, I was used to medical examinations, so when he tried to take my pants off, I protested. I'd never had a doctor touch me like that and try to unzip my jeans and remove them. What kind of doctor takes your clothes off you? I had brought my mom with me, and she was used to helping me don a gown for examination. She had been asked to wait in the lobby. I called out to her, and she helped me out of the office and out of the building.

I was terrified, disgusted, shocked, and affronted. How could the Army employ such a deplorable person? How could such a person "treat" patients? I thought back to one of my step-grandfather John's favorite rhetorical questions. He would ask, "What do they call the person who graduates from medical school with the lowest GPA?" Then he would wait a moment, and give the response, "doctor."

In the end, my discharge took years. By this time, I had sold my car, spent my savings, cashed in my CDs, and sold off my stocks. I was advised that I should hire an attorney to assist with my complicated medical board. I ended up spending any money I had left on an experienced military law attorney from Washington state, where the Medical Board Hearing would be held at Fort Lewis.

Thankfully, he advised us on how to organize the overwhelming amount of documentation needed for the board. It filled several file boxes, and included years of medical treatment files from a bevy of military and civilian physicians from more than one state. There were documents from the National Guard Bureau, the Illinois Army National Guard, and other sources.

To make things even more complicated, I had moved several times in the years since my injury, as one of my homes had flooded several times, and another had burned down. I had been to countless doctors at a number of different hospitals in several different states.

My mom and I sorted through the dozens of file boxes filled with Memorandums for Record, medical notes from various facilities, notes of phone calls, and printouts of the countless emails that had passed back and forth through the airwaves over the course of many years. We organized everything by date and scanned as many documents as we could to the computer's hard drive and then to compact discs. We tried to ensure that the board would have everything they might need, as we of course could not rely on Lemon to provide them with all of the required documentation.

Every time I thought about all of the pain and frustration I had endured, I fell deeper and deeper into depression. If it wasn't for my mother, I would have given up and withdrawn from life.

We flew out the day prior to the hearing and met my attorney at his home office. Over tea and a demonstration of his animatronic miniature tanks, we discussed how he felt the hearing could go. Very few National Guard or Reserve soldiers received a full medical discharge. Yes, I was injured while on active duty, but it was for training, which was apparently a sticky point, as I was not part of a force multiplier in a war.

The hearing was held in a large office with a conference table, behind which three Army Officers sat. One medical officer, an attorney, and another individual of officer rank had reviewed my file and had spoken with the local JAG officer and my attorney prior to my arrival. I had not worn a uniform in years and felt utterly awkward. The three men sitting behind the long table would decide my future, and they intimidated me. Although it was common to stand at attention in front of a board, my condition dictated that we sit.

I was very happy I had my own attorney! We had gone over the barrage of medical documents prior to even showing up at the hearing. A JAG officer who would have been assigned my case took a look at the size of the medical file under our attorney's arm, did the sign of the cross as though blessing him, and walked out.

The hearing took about an hour and a half, which I felt was rather short to take the life of a soldier into account and submit a decision that would be etched in stone forever. I received a medical discharge, and was permanently medically relieved of my duties.

The board thanked me for my service, and I broke down and cried. The board members were very nice, but they did have one really odd comment. They said that they had never seen such inappropriate and derogatory comments made in a discharge packet as those made by Lemon. They said they wanted it recorded that disciplinary action should be taken against Lemon for his unprofessional behavior. I'm not sure if anything was ever done about that. I can only hope that no one else suffered from his lack of empathy and unprincipled behavior.

After serving for six and half years enlisted, another two as an officer, and then barely keeping my head above water while on TDRL and waiting and wondering what was wrong with me, it was all over. I was overwhelmed, sad, and relieved. I was grieving the loss of my career and uncertain about my future. All I knew at this point was that I needed to apply for benefits with the Veterans Administration and continue my medical care at the Edwards Hines, Jr. VA hospital.

LITA & JEAN

22

LITA: REINFORCEMENTS

SOMETIME DURING THE EARLY PART of the last eighteen months, I transferred to the United States Transportation Command (USTRANSCOM) at Scott Air Force Base, located in St. Clair County, Illinois, about 15 miles east of St. Louis. I had made it to the rank of major while at the Eighty-Fifth, and there were no positions for me to take at my new rank.

After a short search within the Army Reserves, I found a transportation officer position that was mobilizing upon entry to the unit due to the post 9/11 troop buildup in Iraq. Most of the Main Operating Bases (MOBs) were stateside, one right there at Scott AFB, just four and a half hours from my home in Illinois.

Jean was undergoing therapies and there wasn't much I could do to help with that, so I took the position, bought a thirty-one-foot camper, and moved to Scott. I lived at the fam-camp on base at the end of a runway. Our assignment was four days on and three days off with eighteen-hour days. This was tiring to say the least, but it was massively exciting!

Our office looked like something out of a movie set, with

big-screen monitors surrounding the command center where all of the armed services had branch reps serving to assist in the movement of goods and troops. I was a lowly major amongst lieutenant colonels, colonels, generals, and daily briefings with the Central Command (CENTCOM) Commander and the Secretary of Defense (SECDEF). I worked with computer programs that would ensure a seamless transfer of personnel from the Continental United States (CONUS) to the theater of engagement.

At one meeting, in which I was the lowest ranking officer, a question about a specific type of vehicle came up. The star-studded group all turned to me, the transportation officer, asking for more details about the vehicle. I was clueless! I knew it was a very large and very powerful vehicle, but that's about it. So I furrowed my brow and nodded knowingly, stating, "Oh, yes, that's the BAT."

The generals all nodded back at me. Then one asked, what does BAT stand for?

"Well, sir," I said, "it stands for Big Ass Truck." There followed another series of nods and a few snickers.

My best times were at the beginning and the end. I had accepted the challenge the Army gave me and had taken the lessons learned throughout my time in the service, culminating in a high level position, with a temporary status of a top secret clearance, which allowed me to see the bigger picture of warfare on a global level. The security clearances were taking longer than normal due to the huge influx of personnel being investigated now that the war was in full swing. I was able to work in the position while waiting on the security investigation. I enjoyed working with members of the Army, Navy, Air Force, Coast Guard, and Marines. We were an integrated team working toward a common goal. Together, we ensured that we had boots on the ground and supplies to support our troops, no matter where they were.

I worried somewhat that my arrest from long ago might come back to bite me. I checked myself and found the record had been expunged, but I wasn't sure how that would be evaluated for this.

It was around this time that the Chicago Archdiocese settled a class action lawsuit with victims of abuse, including me. They publicly apologized, named Pete as a perpetrator, and admitted wrongdoing. Although I was glad that they finally were acknowledging it, I was also saddened by the decades of the Archdiocese refuting claims and simply shuffling abusive priests from one church to the next. They still in 2022 have no central or anonymous means by which someone may lodge a complaint. They tell people to go to their local law enforcement for assistance.

Concurrently, I had to help Jean with her medical problems back in Chicago. I thoroughly enjoyed the work I was doing at USTRANSCOM and felt like I was performing an essential duty to my country, but with the pending security investigation and my daughter's injuries, I felt that my next war should be fought at home, so I tendered my resignation.

Four years earlier, in April of 2000, I had received a call from my daughter's unit at Ft. Leonard Wood, informing me that she was injured and in the hospital. Within an hour, my husband and I were driving to Rolla, Missouri, six hours away. Upon our arrival early the next morning, I was relieved to see Jean sitting up in the hospital bed. She had a neck brace on and a sling over her left shoulder, but looked OK, perhaps just a bit tired, but we all did. Then the doctor who was rounding on his patients gave us an update.

"Jean will be fine," he said. "She was injured in a high jump during a training exercise and suffered a cervical sprain and shoulder tendinitis." He was just then releasing her from the hospital.

Again relieved, with a full day before the end of cycle ceremony, we checked Jean out and drove her back to her apartment. Since she was very sore, we packed up her personal belongings and made plans to drive her, her gear, and her car home the next day after the ceremony. It was time for me to hang up the uniform and stand by Jean.

For the next four years, she would undergo therapies and surgeries that proved fruitless, and her health was deteriorating. Once again, I felt totally useless as a mom. What could I do to help her? I searched for answers everywhere I could.

I researched her symptoms myself and came to the conclusion that she needed more than she was getting in physical therapy. I asked her unit to transfer her care to a neurologist. I was denied. I asked friends and acquaintances who were still in the service what my options were. I had never experienced this type of problem in my entire career. I had never known of anyone who had gone through such an experience, and I felt like I was battling it alone.

One friend, a Captain in the Navy still working at USTRANSCOM, suggested that I write to my Congressman. The thought of my early days and cutting grass with scissors after a casual meeting between Congressman Henry Hyde and my good friend Bob Lillard came roaring back in my mind. "YES!" I knew that was the answer! Congressional interference was more feared by the command structure than any foreign enemy! I immediately made an appointment to meet with both our local Congressman and Senator. I don't recall what response we received from the Congressional Representative, but I do recall Senator Obama's assistant saying we could leave the letter and he would see what could be done.

That letter must have been the magic bullet, because there was now a great deal of attention being placed on Jean Marie's medical condition, and a new target on my head. I didn't care about the fury I obviously raised in the command structure. I was used to it, and Jean was now able to be seen by a civilian neurologist of our choosing. This was still just the beginning of the fight, however.

23

JEAN: A VETERAN'S AFFAIRS

WITH A DISABILITY DISCHARGE FOR a Line of Duty injury while on Active Duty, I was eligible for health care at any VA health care facility. The process for getting a disability pension, a monthly payment, was far more difficult.

Supposedly, all I had to do was fill out a form. Then a medical specialist would review my file, examine me, and submit his or her findings. In reality, it wasn't at all easy. The process is difficult. You have to be extremely detailed on the forms. If you leave off a condition, symptom, or diagnosis, it will not be evaluated or rated. Every condition is given a percentage based on severity. The percentages can exceed 100. I still don't have a handle on the whole thing.

At Hines, the office for rating evaluations is very hard to reach. It is at the opposite end of the main entrance, down weird windowless corridors, through narrow doorways, through an indoor garden, and up a tiny elevator. If you park by the main entrance or use the valet service, you're in for a hike.

In the office, things get even stranger. The individuals who examined me never introduced themselves. They would call my name, walk down to their office, and indicate that I should enter. I have no idea if they were qualified to examine me. They might have been administrators, doctors, or data entry personnel. No "Hi, I'm Dr. So and So, and I'll be conducting your rating evaluation." Nothing. It was really unnerving and impersonal. I received my rating evaluation packet in the mail and was surprised by all of the things that were not included or evaluated. It took time to get everything ironed out.

The process for applying for health care was actually very easy. I walked a copy of my discharge paperwork, LOD, and ID to a processing desk in the ER at Hines. Then I was told that I could set up an appointment with a physician. Because I am a woman, I was told that my primary care provider would be an OBGYN in the basement of the hospital. I didn't have any issues requiring an OBGYN; I needed a neurologist, an orthopedist, and care from someone in mental health. The OBGYN clinic was creepy. People walking by would constantly stop and stare into the porthole window at the patients waiting. The whole office felt like an afterthought.

Around this time, my parents decided that I would be living with them permanently, and decided to move. They found a rather rundown mansion, built in the 1970s, in the Brook Forest subdivision in Oak Brook, Illinois. We called it the "Poltergeist House." The 3,800 square foot home had more than enough room for my mom, my stepfather, and me. We each had our own bedroom and bathroom. I had my own floor.

The garden for this home was divided into five distinct areas. To the South was a pond and a small apple orchard. At the center of the back yard was an in-ground pool with a slide and diving board and a small pool house. During the summer, we were constantly removing frogs and shooing mallard ducks out of this pool. To the west of the pool was a small lawn.

North of the pool was a rather odd area. It was six feet higher than the rest of the yard, covered in ivy and weeds, and with a huge chain-link cage at one end. To the east of the pool was a large sunken garden with a separate lawn and paved patio area.

We've always enjoyed growing our own vegetables, and within a month of moving in, my mom was laying out a vegetable garden—that is, until one of our neighbors, Nancy, poked her head over the fence and told us that we might want to get our vegetables at the farmers market instead. A number of homes on our block and a section of Midwest Road had been built right over a nineteenth century Thurston Settlers' Cemetery. They had removed the headstones but had left the bodily remains in the ground.

When Nancy had work done in her yard in 2001, a worker dug up a human skull. No one had informed her, or us, that the homes were built over a cemetery!

We squashed our hopes for homegrown vegetables and contacted an archeologist from the University of Illinois. He arrived one day with his young son and ground radar to assess the situation.

We had already put money into brand-new kitchen appliances, cleaning the two-foot-deep muck out of the pool, and putting in a new pool pump and filter and various safety items. Then we learned that it would cost more than thirty thousand dollars to excavate the remains and have them reburied elsewhere. Whew!

We were renting this property and wanted to do the right thing, but without any support from the homeowners, the cost was more than we could undertake. Since the owners, who just happened to live at the end of the block, did not maintain the property, it had several extremely degraded and dangerous areas. The balcony and deck above the patio was rotting through, and the railing was there in name only.

With 3,800 square feet, and three floors, I had the lower-level walkout with my own kitchen, office, living room, bedroom, a huge steam room, and even a sunken garden, which gave me a sense of independence. My bathroom was compact, with a cast-iron tub along the back wall, a toilet and single sink to the right, and a towel rack to the left.

The floor above was the main living area. It included another full eat-in kitchen, dining room, guest bathroom, and large living room. The living room was retro fabulous! The original wraparound cabinetry included a hidden bar and entertainment system. The upper floor included four more bedrooms and two bathrooms.

Unfortunately, this meant that my mom was two floors up from me at night, so anytime I needed help, I would have to wait for her to get to me.

Very early one morning, around three a.m., I got up to go to the bathroom. I peed, washed my hands, and turned around to dry my hands. Then everything went dark and apparently my parents, asleep two floors up, heard a loud thump, and the whole house shook. Next thing I remember, I was head down in the bathtub. My head, neck, and left knee hurt! Blood ran down my face, and tears formed in my eyes. I had just had yet another syncopal episode. This time, I had fractured my cribriform plate, had a CSF leak, and had chipped my kneecap. To help the CSF leak heal, I was put on complete bed rest.

That Christmas, my mother gave me an amazing gift that really lifted my spirits. Yep, an empty box. She said her gift to me was a bit "out of the box." My mom was giving the gift of life in my honor. She had gone on a website called MatchingDonors. com, and registered to donate a kidney. She still felt bad for me since I was not able to donate bone marrow years before, and she had been looking for an opportunity to donate. She had heard about a retired firefighter, Rodney Flemming, from Southern Illinois, who desperately needed a kidney donation. She would be donating one of her kidneys to him. The procedure went well for both of them and my mom made a new lifelong friend.

Unfortunately, my own health continued to be problematic. My mother's concern grew every time I blacked out. Every time I tried to stand up, I found that I was falling down. I fell one day while walking the dog and tore the tendons off my ankle, which required a surgical repair and more hardware.

All the while I was still going to physical therapy and occupational therapy at Hines. The physical therapy department was crammed into the basement, along with the TBI clinic and obstetrics and gynecology. In addition to my twice weekly sessions at PT and OT, I had to do exercises at home on my own. I was determined to regain my strength and push through. Tears rolled down my face every time I tried to brush my hair or teeth with my left arm. The pain was overwhelming. I would sob as I tried to pull on my pants and socks. My physical therapist said that I wasn't working hard enough, that she could see a gap on my back where muscle should be. She told me to work harder. I did. I felt like a failure, and withdrew further from the people around me.

At family parties, my aunts and uncles would ask when I was going to get better, or if I was better already, as if I had a cold that would simply go away. They would give me hard excruciatingly painful pats on my back, right where my shoulder blade surgery was, despite my asking repeatedly that they not do so. My uncles took pains to inform me that they watched videos of people in Africa doing the high jump, with no mats at all, and that those people were just fine. I felt as if they were trying to imply that I should be fine. One of my aunts told me that she knew people who were dying and that they were happier than me. Maybe death was the way out. Maybe. I stopped going out, going to parties, going to the store, or anywhere else.

After years of physical therapy with no improvement, I went to the orthopedics department at Hines. There, the surgeon said that my shoulder was fine because my collarbone wasn't fractured. This was new to me. I wasn't sure what my collarbone had to do with my shoulder blade, but okay. It was dawning on me that most "shoulder doctors" worked on the shoulder joint and not the shoulder blade.

My mom started to wonder about the gap on my back. After all, every doctor pointed it out to her as an indication that there was no muscle development. Then Mom found a specialist in Lexington, Kentucky, by the name of Kibler. Dr. Kibler specialized in scapular injuries and treated some of the world's most elite athletes. Off Mom and I went to Lexington, passing Fort Knox on the way.

Dr. Kibler is a no-nonsense, quick-to-the-answer man, and when he had me lift my arm, he motioned my mother over to see what he was seeing. "Watch this. Look here," he coached her as I raised and lowered my arm. "Do you see how this indents right here? It shouldn't do that. I can fix it. I see it all the time."

He explained to us how the muscles in my back were detached, or torn off. As it turned out the muscle, tendons, and ligaments had torn off of my scapula, and it was no longer working as it should.

No matter how hard I pushed myself at PT or OT, the muscle could not reattach and heal on its own. Dr. Kibler had invented a procedure to repair it. He actually toured the country explaining his procedure at medical conferences so that others could follow his lead in repairing this type of injury! Because of the tears, the scapula rested against my rib cage and grated, so the procedure that had been performed in Chicago wasn't enough. My recovery couldn't really start until after those muscles were reattached. Dr. Kibler said he could drill holes along the edge of the scapula and reattach the infraspinatus muscle that was hanging loose and no longer working. After getting all of this information, we returned home and spoke with the orthopedic surgeon at Hines. We wanted to let him know what we had learned and see if he could perform the procedure, as I only had medical coverage through the VA. He said that he didn't want to hear another doctor's opinion and would not do anything to treat me. I was at a loss. Everyone said they could see the gap on my back where the muscle should have been. Did they really think it was due to a lack of effort? I felt deflated, angry, and frustrated.

24

JEAN: ONE STEP FORWARD . . .

MY MOM HAD STAYED IN touch with several of my friends, including James, the Major I had dated prior to my injury. I think it helped that she had run into him previously.

I had gone to the movies with James when I got back from OBC, but I was in so much pain that we had to cut the date short. Over the years, I had withdrawn into a deep depression, and had lost touch with James, along with everyone else I once called a friend.

Life had moved on for James, but my mom still hung out with him. James had not only organized his collection of military books, but also had founded the Pritzker Military Museum and Library (PMML). He had donated meteors to the Adler Planetarium and dedicated an exhibit to his father.

By this time, James had also decided to transition from a man to woman, and would now be known as Jennifer. Jennifer is a wonderful, extremely intelligent, and kind person. If she was happier and more comfortable, we wholeheartedly supported her transition. Now I understood the dress comment she made on our first date, and I still regret the misunderstanding. Jennifer is such an amazing, interesting, and thoughtful person that I think I would have liked her no matter what, and I wish I could have made her more comfortable in that early moment.

In her outreach to everyone she knew, my mom had told Jennifer about my situation. The orthopedic surgeon in Kentucky said that my shoulder muscles were detached and needed to be surgically reattached. At the time, I did not have insurance and relied on the Veterans Administration for care related to my injuries. If I wanted to have the procedure, I would have to pay out of pocket, and my financial resources had been exhausted long ago.

Jennifer said that she would pay for the procedure and physical therapy afterwards. I was shocked and confused. I also felt bad for having to get financial assistance from anyone. I would be forever indebted to Jennifer, and didn't see how I could ever repay her kindness.

I had no idea that Jennifer was wealthy until this point. When we were chatting online, I was just thrilled to come across someone who was so intelligent, understood my military background, and had been in a relationship before. Money didn't really matter to me. I was still in college, working full-time, and in the ILARNG. I didn't want or need anyone to support me. I wanted someone to spend time with and with whom I shared interests.

My mom called Dr. Kibler, and we scheduled my surgery for the first available slot.

Dr. Kibler successfully performed the procedure at the local hospital in Lexington, Kentucky. My recovery was slow, and continues to this day. I have been told that it takes nerves twice to three times as long to heal compared to the amount of time that there was an injury or break in connectivity. A decade of unrepaired nerve pain can mean 30 years of continued pain as the nerves slowly heal. But at least we are moving in the right direction!

After the difficulty with care at the VA, I knew I had to do something. I had not yet applied for Social Security benefits or Medicare insurance. It seemed like applying for benefits meant that I was giving up, that I would never work again, and that I had somehow failed. But I needed to be able to get medical care outside of the VA system. I needed to have options available, so I applied and was able to get both Medicare and Tricare insurance. Now my care outside of the VA would be 100% covered. This was a huge relief.

I was still blacking out, fainting, and collapsing several times a day, so I headed to a civilian neurologist with my new health insurance for a visit. They put in requests for another series of MRIs, a CT scan with and without contrast, and a lumbar puncture to test my spinal fluid pressure. With a complete battery of test results at his disposal, the neurologist now came up with two new diagnoses: craniocervical instability with brain stem compression. The doctors called it a bowling ball effect.

My skull had settled down toward my shoulders due to the laxity of the ligaments of the spine. The spinal instability could have been from my accident and a condition called Ehlers-Danlos Syndrome, or EDS. I had never heard of Ehlers-Danlos Syndrome before. It's a hereditary disorder affecting connective tissue. The most severe symptoms arise in the most mobile part of the spine, the craniocervical junction.

Craniocervical instability, I soon found out, was also known as Syndrome of Occipitoatlantoaxial Hypermobility. Apparently, it is a form of structural instability of the craniocervical junction that may lead to a pathological deformation of the brainstem, upper spinal cord, and cerebellum. The permanent solution was yet another surgery: a craniocervical fusion where rods would be connected from my skull to my vertebrae.

By this time, I was tired of doctors and hospitals, and sick of being injured. I didn't want another surgery. I didn't want more PT and OT. I just wanted this all to be over already. In the interim,

I would have to wear a neck brace to lift and stabilize my injury.

My new GP at Hines sent me to the prosthetics lab, where I was fitted with a Neck Chest Head Brace Cervical Thoracic Orthosis that I essentially lived in for the next six months. The brace was a system of steel bars, a helmet, and chest and back plates covered in white plastic. The helmet wrapped around my skull and clipped under my chin, physically lifting my head up. I looked like a broken science fiction combat droid. My nephews thought it was fantastic, and they all wanted their own braces. I was not as thrilled and more than a little uncomfortable. I had started to gain weight and had to have the brace enlarged twice before I was simply too large to wear it.

From there I switched to an Aspen Vista Collar without the thoracic support, which held my head and neck immobile, but was less restrictive and cumbersome. At this time, I was finally seen at the Traumatic Brain Injury Clinic at Hines. The first doctor I saw in the clinic said that I didn't need to be there, as I didn't have a TBI. This was news to me. I had hit my head. I had lost consciousness. I had had brain surgery. I was waiting to have more brain surgery. But I didn't have a Traumatic Brain Injury? Okay, then.

After wearing a brace for over a year, I finally gave in and agreed to have the craniocervical fusion procedure. The physician pioneering this procedure performed it at a hospital in Great Neck, New York. *Great Neck! Of all places!* We flew to New York and had a few consultations with Dr. Bolognese. I ended up sleeping through all of the drama during the procedure. A resident was assisting and he cut through an artery in my brain. I bled out and coded. Luckily, Dr. Bolognese stepped in and acted quickly. He repaired the damage, and I was given bags of O negative donor blood and revived.

When I learned that I had coded, that my mother and sister had been told what had happened by a crying physician, and that they had been through such a stressful ordeal, I was heartbroken. I felt heavily that I had not endured the years of pain, depression, and stress alone. Despite having intentionally or unintentionally pushed everyone away, my mother and sister were my constant cheerleaders.

I now had complete support of my cranium, and my brain stem was no longer smashed in half. With any luck, my parasympathetic nervous system would repair itself.

After this second neurosurgery, my mom decided what we needed was a smaller house so that she could keep a closer eye on me. She was tired of running down two flights of stairs every time she heard a loud thud!

After a rather exhaustive search, she found a two-story farmhouse built in 1927 on an acre lot in Downers Grove. The owners of the property were living out of state, and the house had fallen into disrepair. A storm had knocked down a stand of trees. One had even crashed through the garage roof. We had the mass of fallen trees removed.

Meanwhile, the kitchen was a 1980s nightmare! White melamine cabinets with oak trim! The horror! We could live with the bad design, but the broken glass bottles in the broken garbage disposal and piles of sand in the washing machine were more of a challenge to overcome.

The first-floor bathroom was an odd, poorly executed do-it-yourself project. The countertops were MDF plywood covered in a mosaic tile with wide grout lines that soaked in water like a sponge. We had to repair the large holes in the shower walls and tried to ignore the tiles falling off the nonworking fireplace and popping up off of the sunroom floor.

The day we moved in, my dog, Gigi, made quite an impression on our new neighbors. We adopted her from a shelter. She's a large mixed breed dog, part soft-coated wheaten terrier, part Great Dane, part Chow, part mop. Well, no, not really part mop.

But she looks like a mop or a sheepdog from a cartoon. She joined the family when I was on bed rest. I would see a fluffy white tail circling my bed like a shark's fin. Then she'd jump up and playfully bite my hand. So we started calling her the Great White Gremlin, or GG for short.

The day we moved into the new house, Gigi grabbed an open box of tampons off of the bathroom floor and ran outside with them. Gigi proceeded to throw tampons up in the air one at a time as we chased after her. It looked as if we had taught Gigi the oddest trick ever! She had never done this before, or since, and I'm grateful it was a one-time adventure. We met our new neighbors as we gathered up the tampons strewn all over the yard.

The neighbors owned the two-acre lot with a spring fed-pond just north of us, where they raised turkeys and worked in a home woodshop. We would wake up each morning to find turkeys looking down at us from the neighbors' roof.

The neighbor across the street came over to welcome us to the area. He was an older man who introduced himself as a retired hitman. He said that he had done his time, but was willing to take on the odd job if we ever needed that sort of thing. I don't know if he was serious or not.

Our house needed a lot of work. We had to have the railing on the poorly constructed back porch reinforced, and several broken steps replaced as well. We did like the potting room, lean-to greenhouse, and wall-to-wall, floor to ceiling, built-in cabinetry in the dining room!

At any rate, yet again we were in the uncomfortable position of renting a home from owners who had no interest in maintaining the property. The basement flooded three times. Heavy rains and inadequate exterior drainage had caused two of the floods, and the homeowners had caused the last flood! They had purchased a damaged washing machine to replace the sand-filled one. The water did not turn off when the washing machine tub was filled.

The washing machine continued to fill and overflow all day while we were at the hospital. We returned home to a basement full of water, our stored items destroyed, and our spare full-size freezer full of food melting in a basement that wasn't safe to enter for a few days. I was despondent! I was so tired of flooding houses. The homeowners didn't seem to care about us or the house.

My mom again contacted Jennifer, who, with the help of her property company rolled into our lives like an Abrams Tank. All guns were loaded, and we had a definite feeling of security with this support.

Jennifer was a lifesaver. She went beyond what we could have dreamed of for help. She negotiated with the absentee landlord to end our lease and found a one-floor ranch for my mom and me to live in. She even had the new house completely modified for my mobility concerns. Her contractors widened doorways, added beautiful grab bars in the bathrooms, raised toilets, put in insulation, made roof repairs, raised the vegetable garden, updated the lighting, and added drainage and an endless list of accommodations to make life livable. We will be forever grateful and indebted to this amazing woman!

Unfortunately, however, a change in living conditions was not enough to pull me out of my deep depression. I felt alone and like a useless burden.

And to make matters worse, my mom and I were suddenly having daily disagreements. I would make a suggestion. My mom would shoot it down. A few days later, my mom would say that she had a great idea, my idea from before. She was presenting my ideas back to me as though they were her shiny new ideas. She would get agitated at the drop of a hat and was very snappish. Sometimes I had difficulty understanding what she was saying. I didn't know what was going on. Was she messing with me? Was she gaslighting me? Why was she doing this?

It was an emotionally painful period. One week we were not

on speaking terms. I spent the week in bed, only getting up to take sips of water. I didn't eat. I didn't talk with anyone. At the end of the week, I gave up and took two handfuls of my prescription sleeping pills. I thought that was it, I would pass away in my sleep. No more pain. No more stress. No more me.

I did not die. I got a really good night's sleep and slept straight through until the next evening.

I guess my mom knew her behavior was off as well. She went to her doctor, saw several specialists, and had CAT scans, blood tests, and MRIs done. It turned out she had early onset Alzheimer's. Although I was relieved to know what was going on with my mom, I was also saddened by the news. My mom is one of the most intelligent people I have ever met. Now her mind would slowly fail her. She would begin to forget and become more and more dependent on the care of others. We resolved that we would spend as much time as possible with friends and family.

25
LITA: A HINT FROM BOSTON IN NORTH CAROLINA

AFTER THOSE TWO YEARS OF no relief for Jean, I was tired of the often ineffective, painful, and dangerous medical advice. I took things into my own hands, searched the internet, and found a physician in Lexington, Kentucky who worked with professional sports participants who had scapular injuries.

We drove down to his office, and within one minute he made me cry. He looked at Jean's upper back where the infraspinatus muscle attaches to the edge of the scapula and said, "I see this all the time. I actually invented a process for repair that I teach other surgeons around the country."

I just bawled! The tears of relief were a stress release valve that just would not stop. His nurse brought me a cup of water, and guided me to a chair where I could sit and compose myself. The nurse handed me a box of tissues and walked back out, closing the door behind her.

I wish I could say the actual surgeries were uneventful, but they weren't. As Jean detailed, the cranio-cervical fusion operation started out with a disaster when a resident accidentally cut an artery in Jean's neck, causing an immediate loss of most of her blood supply, making her flatline, and requiring the operating team to push blood back into her at a frantic pace to bring her back. I was terrified.

Up next: the scapular surgery. It wouldn't have happened at all if it weren't for Jennifer Pritzker. We returned to Chicago with Dr. Kibler's recommendation and tried in vain to convince the military medical review board to authorize the surgery. The physician's assistant who did the review and refusal was adamant that if the clavicle wasn't broken, she did not need any other surgeries. I wrote to our Congressional representatives again, but did not hear back. All I could do was revert to the same tears I had shed in the doctor's office in Kentucky, but these were tears of fear, hopelessness, and empathy for Jean now that we knew what the problem was and that we were unable to do anything about it.

I reached out to the same friends in the military I had gone to over the years for advice, including Jennifer.

I was sitting in Jennifer's kitchen having a second cup of excellent freshly ground brew, giving the latest update on Jean, when Jennifer asked how she could help. I initially thought maybe she would contact someone we hadn't, so I easily and eagerly said, "Yes, please, anything you can think of would be great!"

Her idea of helping went further than I dreamed. She actually contacted the doctor's office and hospital where the surgery would take place, and paid for the entire procedure! Some people merely say they support the veterans, but trust me, this woman lives those words.

The surgery was completed in the next few months. The surgeon drilled a number of small holes in her scapula and carefully reattached each band of muscle to the new anchor points. The recovery was long for both operations, and she still has autonomic issues with her breathing, heart rate, blood pressure, and digestion as well as pain. With the ratio of time injured to time healed being three to one, it might be another thirty years before she is completely healed.

Once Jean's surgeries were in the rearview mirror, I knew that it was time to focus on the future. A soldier loves to have a clear mission statement, and loves to train. An officer's training revolves around planning.

My love of planning would come in very handy throughout my life. I was diagnosed with early onset Alzheimer's after noticing I couldn't remember recent events, or work with numbers. The PET Scan showed amyloid plaque in my brain. That, together with a series of other tests results, convinced everyone of the diagnosis.

I was crushed and relieved at the same time. I did want to know what was going on and why I wasn't functioning as sharply as I once did, but Alzheimer's has a terminal aspect.

I was now bound and determined to do what I could to keep my mind sharp. That was part of the impetus of this book, to get my story out, to work those brain cells harder than they wanted to, and to go back down memory lane to see what I could and could not remember. This book has been part of my therapy.

In July of 2017, Jean and I were at Duke Medical Center in Durham, North Carolina, for an intensive doctor-supervised health, wellness, exercise, and weight loss program. We decided to stay for three months, so we packed up the minivan and the pups and headed east.

Jean had found a three-bedroom, three-bath, two-story townhouse in an all-rental subdivision not far from Duke. My grandson, Sean, drove out with us to help us unpack and settle in.

The day we moved in, we noticed people moving in right next door. We waved and called out a greeting.

"How are you?" asked a tall, spritely woman in her early fifties as she toted boxes down the driveway. It seemed more of a statement than a question, so I replied with a simple "Hello."

As if she was waiting for this slightest of human contact,

acknowledgement, or affirmation, she quickly ran up to us as we stood on either side of the minivan, all doors open. "Are you here for a transplant? They're just so great, right?"

Again, the words that were formed appeared to imply a question with the expectation of a response, but she quickly added, "We're here for a liver. My friend, she needs the liver."

Where was this lady from? I couldn't place the strong accent, but I guessed it was from the New England area. Jean moved across the grass separating our driveways and watched the movers unload our neighbors' boxes while Sean unloaded our minivan. I stayed in conversation with our new neighbor. Jean had overheard what the neighbor had said about Duke being 'so great' for liver transplants and quickly started doing research on her phone to determine why this particular hospital network had an advantage.

We had barely finished with some initial pleasantries when Jean called to me and said, "Mom, we have to call your cousin with liver failure!"

My cousin had been diagnosed with liver failure a few months after her father, my Uncle Butch, received his own terminal diagnosis. Uncle Butch had died the year before after refusing a liver transplant. Now his daughter was dying from the same condition and had recently received a month to live. Although she sat on the United Network for Organ Sharing (UNOS)'s waiting list for over a year, they didn't have much hope for her.

"Duke *specializes* in organ transplants!" Jean quickly explained. They take livers and cut them to form mirror images and are then able to transplant them to twice as many patients. They actually send teams out to physically evaluate organs, rather than turning down a possibly viable organ simply because of a description on a piece of paper. They do "hot box" transplants. This means they keep warm blood pumping through organs, giving them a longer transplant window. There was also a high percentage of people with type A blood types, my cousin's blood type, living in the Raleigh-Durham area.

For all of these reasons, our new neighbors had driven all the way down from Boston for a liver transplant. Boston! That was the accent I couldn't place!

I stopped unpacking, sat down in the living room on a comfortable couch in this fully furnished townhouse, and scoured the internet. It did appear to be true. Unpacking could wait. I needed a break anyway.

After letting the dogs back into the house, I yelled upstairs to Jean, "Road trip!"

"What? Why? No! We just got here!" she complained.

"I just want to swing by the hospital and find out about this transplant business," I replied.

The two of us took off for the main hospital in the Duke Medical complex fifteen minutes away. It was easy to find the liver transplant department. This place was so big into transplants they actually had entire departments for each organ! Long story short, they acknowledged what the neighbor had said, and yes, they would evaluate my cousin as a possible patient.

I called my cousin, and explained what we had just found out at Duke. I told her to pack a bag. We were going to fly her out to North Carolina, and she could stay with us. A week later, my cousin landed at Raleigh-Durham International Airport, and a month after that, she was on the road to recovery with a new liver. My cousin went from a jaundiced young mother of two teenagers, already at peace with her situation and resigned that she wouldn't live more than a few weeks, to a happy, vibrant mom who saw her daughter go to prom and her oldest graduate from high school.

Prior to this experience at Duke, neither Jean nor I knew how to care for a recent transplant patient. We learned all we could from frequent conversations with our new neighbor, who had her transplant a month before my cousin's. Online support groups for organ transplant patients quickly got us up to speed.

We assured my cousin that we would do everything we could to keep her healthy.

My sister Mary flew out to help give the rental property a deep cleaning, as my cousin would be susceptible to illness after her transplant. Her teenage daughters flew out to lend emotional support, as did her mother and brother. We all pulled together to do whatever we could to support my cousin. My cousin told us that watching the neighbor's rapid recovery let her know that there was hope.

Once we were all back at home, it dawned on me that there were other people out there who could use peer to peer support. A platform such as a podcast would be a perfect delivery tool, as we could talk with people about their healthcare journeys. We could find out what they wished they and their families had known, and what helped them the most with their recovery. One day, over dinner, I said, "Jean, I think we should create a podcast."

26

JEAN: THE NEXT DIAGNOSIS

MY MOTHER WANTS TO DO a podcast? My immediate response was, "Mom, have you ever even listened to a podcast?"

"Hmm, no, but I get the idea, and the idea is enough for me," she said.

I was constantly telling her about something interesting I had heard on a podcast. But now she wanted to start one? It seemed like a steep hill. I explained my objections: we have no technical knowledge. We had no recording equipment. We have very similar voices. I figured we'd be terrible podcast hosts.

A few days later, Mom said, "I've got a male voice." That kind of threw me a little bit.

"Mom, you have a very high female voice," I responded, looking at her askance.

"No, no, I found a male voice," my mom said with excitement.

"What are you talking about?' I asked, wondering what was going on.

"For the podcast, I found a male voice for the podcast!"

"—oh right, the podcast!" I said.

Ron Rispoli, someone my mom went to graduate school with, has a deep male voice. He is a certified recreational therapist and works with special education students transitioning out of the school system. Although COVID put a damper on his Paralympics Archery dreams for 2020, he hopes to participate in the next Olympic cycle.

My mom told Ron about her idea for a patient advocate podcast. We would talk with a new person every week.

My mom named our podcast "PodcastDX," not realizing that you do not need to include the word "Podcast" in the title of your show. But she had already set up our online presence in that name, recruited another host, and offered a convincing pitch, so I went with it, and I'm glad I did.

That is how PodcastDX (DX is the abbreviation for "diagnosis") came into being.

As of 2022, we are now well into our eighth season. Each week, we interview a different person and cover a different diagnosis. For the first episode, my mom took a portable recorder down to Sullivan, Illinois, to interview her "kidney buddy," Rod Fleming, to whom she had donated a kidney in 2010, and his sister Danell.

We did the second podcast with my cousin, who continues to make a remarkable recovery! We've had the chance to talk with people and have followers from all over the globe. We're especially proud of our interviews with military veterans.

We were able to interview Travis Mills, Army war veteran and quad amputee; Seth Kastle, a veteran with PTSD who has written a series of children's books about it; Kristal Kent and Norman Hanley, both military veterans with fibromyalgia and patient advocates; and Brian Tally, a veteran who wrote the Tally Bill which we hope will help future veterans.

The other day, my mother and I were at my sister's house, ostensibly to visit her flock, which includes six chickens and two ducks. The three of us decided to drive over to a local hardware store and pick up a few items that would improve the security of the chicken run. We put on our face masks, in adherence to Covid-19 health regulations, and headed to the store. My sister drove our mother's minivan, I sat shotgun, and our mom sat in the back. When we got back to my sister's house and her boys had unloaded the van, we started to head back to the chicken coop. Since my sister had parked on the street, I wanted to make sure she had the van keys and had locked the vehicle. As she stood on one side of the van and I stood on the other, I called out, "Do you have her keys?"

My sister looked across at me, surprised, and screamed back, "No, I don't have herpes!"

Eyes wide, I looked over to my mom, and then back to my sister. "No, no! Do you have her keys?"

My mom looked from one of us to the other, trying to figure out why in the hell we were standing in the street and screaming back and forth at one another.

Kym looked back at me, and with her hands now on her hips she screamed across to me, "Why are you asking if I have herpes? No, I don't have herpes!" as her apparent frustration grew.

"Okay, okay!" I said as I raised one arm in mock surrender. "Please, please stop screaming herpes!" By this time I was wondering what the neighbors were thinking and bent over giggling.

Our days are not easy. It's more work than we can handle sometimes. But we have an amazing group of people who help us. Weekly therapy sessions, now conducted via cellular phone, time with family and friends, extremely qualified healthcare providers, and laughter all help us get through the painful rough patches.

27

LITA & JEAN: FINAL THOUGHTS

MOM WENT TO BASIC TRAINING at Fort Jackson, South Carolina. Nearly sixteen years later, I followed in her footsteps. I joined the Army, and by chance also headed to basic training at Fort Jackson.

The U.S. Army may still be a boys' club. I don't know if women in MOS's other than stereotypical office positions are still directed to a typewriter when they arrive at their first duty station, but I hope things have changed. Equality will take time, and we all need to help to balance the field. Things are getting better, but in 2022 women still only make up fifteen or so percent of the active duty Army and less than ten percent of those receiving benefits from the VA.

A great deal of controversy currently exists over bases named after Confederate generals; maybe this would be the time to change them. There are Navy ships named after women, but ships have long been deemed female and are considered so as objects rather than badges of honor.

At Edward Hines, Jr. Hospital, progress has been made.

The newly titled "Women's Health Clinic" is now on the twelfth floor. A wall blocks the view of the patient waiting area from any lookie-loos. The whole area feels warm and inviting, and most of all, intentional. There is even a lactation room. Someone going there today for an appointment would not think that women's healthcare was an afterthought. When they call me back for my appointment in the general medicine clinic, they're less likely to call "Mr. McNamara."

An influx of active female veterans from recent years are changing and challenging the culture in the VA health system. One such woman is Senator Tammy Duckworth, whom my mom and I have seen in prosthetics and high heels, climbing out of her pick-up truck at Hines. She has "walked the walk" after serving and being shot down and severely injured in Iraq where she was a helicopter pilot. She has since moved into politics and served as Department Head of the VA and a State Representative, and now serves as one of our two U.S. Senators.

My mom and I are very different, in everything from personality to appearance. She has hickory-colored eyes, shaggy dark-blond hair, and a mischievous grin. She's always been a petite spitfire. She's quick to laugh, and when she does, she laughs loudly, with lots of life! I'm rather reserved and serious myself. It takes a lot to make me laugh, and even then, it is a quiet, conservative chuckle. I envy my mother's love of life, her ability to let go, and her boisterous laugh.

My mom still tries to go out and save the world, one person at a time. She has trouble denying anyone in need. She's the type of person who would gladly give up her spot on a life raft or help put on your oxygen mask first as the airplane's cabin loses pressure. What I think is all the more admirable is that she never makes a big deal over her contributions. She's never one to seek out praise.

She still stops to assist stranded drivers. Just this past winter, she pulled over to the side of the road and helped a teenager whose car had flipped over and landed upside down in a snowbank.

When one of my mother's friend's apartments flooded recently, displacing three children and three adults, my mom was there. She went out and purchased new bed frames and mattresses. She gathered up a van full of their dirty clothing and hauled it off to the laundromat. She helped them sort their belongings and brought some of her own furniture over to offset their losses.

She's given away food, clothing, and hugs to individuals without homes. She delivered truckloads of goods to Katrina victims.

I'm now the same age my mom was when I was injured. I still, however, feel incredibly immature, naive, and inexperienced. How was she able to handle so much with such aplomb?

I'm glad my mom has had this opportunity to tell her story, before her memories fade. Her early onset Alzheimer's diagnosis is not the death sentence it may have once been. She has responded extremely well to treatments, but we both fear for the day when that is no longer the case.

My injuries ended my military career and my civilian career, and forced me to question my overall life goals. I was no longer an Army officer or college student, and was no longer physically active. When someone would ask me what it is I do for a living, I was at a loss for words. What did I do? Nothing, in my opinion. Bed rest, self-hatred, self-loathing, and self-pity summed up my daily itinerary. For many years, I've felt like a drain on society and my friends and family. I felt like I contributed nothing at all to the world at large, and weight gain lowered my opinion of myself even further. Every single time I've needed to have surgery, I've questioned whether I deserved the care, time, and expense required for the procedure.

Recently, things have changed. Instead of people asking if I'm better yet, they ask about our podcast, or how this book is coming along. I feel like I have purpose, and that I am able to contribute something to my community. Writing this book has not only helped bring my previous accomplishments into relief, it has also brought my mom and me closer together. It's funny and meaningful to read her sections and think to myself, *I've been there*, or *wow, she was so young!*

Reliving all of the pain and frustration of the past has been extremely difficult for me. We've gone through a lot of tissues, mental health counseling, and dark thoughts while working on this book. It's been challenging. It's been cathartic. It's given us a chance to look back at everything we've experienced, accept it as the past, and begin to acknowledge that we have some accomplishments. Thank you for taking the time to read our work. I hope it made you smile, reflect, and maybe even laugh. I hope I've been able to show you there's a path through.

I've gained a great deal of perspective, and I'm working to see that I'm more than a burden. I can inspire, connect, and help others. I'm a veteran, sister, aunt, daughter, podcaster, producer, and a writer. I'm a trailblazer, an advocate, and a survivor.

❊ ❊ ❊

Jean is now held firmly together with bars, screws, and other hardware. Whether her hardware and pain could ever be offset by that gold eagle is something only she can answer, but I am forever grateful for every doctor and friend that ensured her a continued chance to wear it proudly.

My daughter and I have been through the wringer, as they say, but we keep in mind that soldiers who deploy to areas of combat sometimes do not return except with a folded flag.

For my family, thanks to our hard work, and despite the attacks of others, we survived, thrived, and learned from all of the experiences we have endured.

Jean notes that I still try to help others around me, and the apple does not fall far from the tree. I am forever grateful for some of the medical tips Jean learned while at Fort Sam Houston and passed on to me. One such instance actually saved my mother's life!

While Jean was training as a medic in Texas, she observed one of her platoon mates pouring a white powder from a folded piece of paper under his tongue. Thinking the soldier was doing illicit drugs, she called him out on it. He laughed slightly, and explained he was taking headache powder. It was Goody's Powder to be exact, a powdered aspirin/caffeine mixture enclosed in a small fold of paper you can keep in your wallet. He told Jean that the powder worked far quicker than conventional tablets. Once I heard about it, I started using them, and my daughter Kym also uses them with some regularity. I always have one or two in my wallet.

One sunny afternoon my sister, my mother, and I were driving from Elmhurst out to one of my brother's homes in Aurora. My mother in the back seat didn't answer one of my questions as we were talking, so I glanced over my shoulder in her direction. She was sitting there looking straight at me with her mouth slightly open and her lips at an odd angle. She looked a bit confused. I repeated the question and still there was silence. I asked, "Mom, can you talk?" and she still had the blank stare but she did finally shake her head back and forth.

My adrenaline rushing now, I glanced up, realized we were approaching the exit for Edwards Hospital in Naperville. I told my sister, "Mom's having a stroke! Go in my wallet, get the powder out, and help her pour it under her tongue."

She unclipped her seat belt, and leaned over the seat. She did what I asked and tried to reassure our mom we would be at the hospital in less than ten minutes. I dialed the hospital and asked for the ER, explained what happened and how close we were, and what we had already given her.

They only had to keep her overnight. Due to the careful attention and complete knowledge of Jean, the quick action of aspirin, and treatment at the hospital, my mother had no residual effects.

In that incident, as throughout our lives, in the end we came out stronger and more determined than ever to help others. We became advocates for ourselves and others: offense as well as defense. It is imperative to advocate for yourself in the military, as it is "mission first." We learned this lesson late and hope this book will act as a guide for others to keep track of their own health problems, keep records, and if the need arises, stand up for themselves.

From one generation to the next, we saw little progress for women in the military. It was a constant fight for both of us. Perhaps change will come now that there are women like Sen. Duckworth, Lt. General Patricia Horoho, and General Ann E. Dunwoody in leadership positions who can make a difference.

In the military, after a training event or a battle, the leadership sits down to complete an after action report. From this, a packet of information is compiled for future soldiers to use in order to avoid obstacles. These are lessons learned. What I learned during my career and my daughter's career is the following:

Always keep records of any problems you come across, whether they regard financial responsibility, like a property book hand receipt, or physical well-being, as in an injury requiring a LOD. You are but a cog in a wheel, and that wheel will continue to spin without you. Take care of yourself. Stand up for yourself. Ask for help. Tell them you won't get married. Tell them you're not the typist. Tell them to follow procedures. Tell them what you need.

With the help of my family and some very dear friends, especially Jennifer N. Pritzker, Colonel, (IL), ILARNG (Retired), we are privileged to have a positive life ahead of us and to dedicate ourselves to helping others live safely and happily.

Our weekly podcast helps not only the patients around the world who we offer our platform to, but each of us as well. We are more than empathetic to the plight of anyone with a medical condition and are the people you want to call if you ever need an advocate on your side!

As we finish this manuscript I am starting yet another medication to fight the slow ravages of Alzheimer's. Working on our weekly episodes helps keep my mind active, and it also gives us both a new sense of purpose.

Jean and I will continue to salute Old Glory at reveille or retreat until the day when the final tones of taps lay us to rest: Jean with her gold eagle upon her lapel, and me with the Big Red One on mine! HOOAH!

RESOURCES

WE'VE GONE THROUGH A LOT in our lifetime, and we know we're not the only ones to face these fights. Our goal with this book is the same as the goal of our podcast - it's the same as our overarching life goal. We want to help others, and to that end we have compiled the below collection of resources.

While putting together this list, we were disappointed to find many dead links, incomplete websites, and a lack of information. There remains a long way to go in terms of support for these struggles, but there are many groups doing very good work. This is by no means a complete or comprehensive list of resources, but it is a collection of valuable, dedicated organizations that are wonderful resources to their communities.

The following information is accurate to the best of our ability at the time of publishing:

Alzheimer's and Related Dementias Education & Referral Center, National Institute on Aging:

nia.nih.gov/health/alzheimers

U.S. Government funded resource providing information regarding dementia news, patient and caregiver resources, and research.

Alzheimer's Association:

alz.org

A comprehensive site for those who desire information about Alzheimer's disease and dementia.

Army Women's Foundation:

awfdn.org/scholarships/general-information/

Provides grants to women soldiers, past and present, and their lineal descendants to help them attain their educational goals.

Chicago Foundation for Women:

cfw.org/why-women/violence/

Charitable foundation which helps women gain economic security, freedom from violence, and access to health care.

Chicago House:

chicagohouse.org/our-history

Social services for the LGBTQ community with emphasis on those impacted by HIV/AIDS.

Elizabeth Dole Foundation :

elizabethdolefoundation.org/our-programs/

Empowers, supports, and honors our nation's military caregivers; the spouses, parents, family members and friends who care for America's wounded, ill or injured veterans.

Family Advocacy Program: defenselink.mil/fapmip	The Department of Defense program, available at every military installation with families, designated to address domestic abuse, child abuse, and neglect.
Howard Brown Health Center: howardbrown.org/	Fights the disparities in healthcare experienced by lesbian, gay, bisexual, and transgender people through research, education, and the provision of services that promote health and wellness. Provides counseling, support groups, workshops, GED programs, and support for those experiencing intimate partner abuse.
Institute for Veterans and Military Families: ivmf.syracuse.edu/ programs/	Focuses on advancing the post-service lives of the nation's military veterans and their families. Entrepreneurship, career training, community services, higher education.
Lake County Veterans and Family Services : lcvetsfoundation.org/	Offers mental health resources, therapy, veteran employment, legal/financial assistance, and family support, free and confidentially, regardless of discharge status.

National Able Network :

nationalable.org/about/

Gives personalized career support to job seekers from all backgrounds and businesses seeking staffing.

National Domestic Violence Hotline:

1800-799-7233

This hotline offers 24-hour crisis intervention, information about domestic violence, and referrals to local programs. All calls are anonymous and answered by trained counselors.

Partnerships for Action, Voices for Empowerment (PAVE) - STOMP Specialized Training of Military Parents:

wapave.org

Works to give support, training, information, and resources to empower and give voice to individuals, youth and families impacted by disabilities. Workshops specific to military families available.

Pregnancy Loss Support Program:

pregnancyloss.org

Provides free counseling and support for individuals who have experienced a miscarriage, stillbirth, newborn death or termination for fetal anomalies, as well as to women who are pregnant following a loss. Open to all regardless of background, religion, gender and sexual orientation.

Soldier Strong: soldierstrong.org/our-programs/	Its mission is to provide revolutionary technology, innovative advancements, and educational opportunities to veterans to better their lives and the lives of their families. PTSD help, disability and major injury rehab/therapy, continuing education.
Suicide Prevention Resource Center: sprc.org/bpr 1(800)273-8255	A federally supported resource center advancing suicide prevention and capacity building through consultation, training, and resources. 24/7, free and confidential support for people in distress, prevention and crisis resources for you or your loved ones, and best practices for professionals.
The Mission Continues : missioncontinues.org	Connects military veterans with new missions in under-resourced communities. Deploys veteran volunteers to work alongside nonprofit partners and community leaders to improve educational resources, tackle food insecurity, foster neighborhood identity, and more.
WINGS: wingsprogram.com/	Provides housing, integrated services, education and advocacy to end domestic violence.

ABBREVIATIONS &
MILITARY TERMS

ABBREVIATION	DEFINITION
63H	Track vehicle repair
AIT	Advanced Individual Training
APG	Aberdeen Proving Ground
ARNG	Army National Guard
Article 15	A section of the Uniform Code of Military Justice allowing commanders to carry out discretionary punishments without judicial proceedings.
ASVAB	Armed Services Vocational Aptitude Battery, a test to determine interests and abilities, used to help assign a military occupational specialty
AT	Annual Training
AWOL	Absent without leave
basic	Basic Training
BAT	Big Ass Truck, a phrase from Lita
BDUs	Battle dress uniform, currently referred to as ADUs (Army Combat Uniform)
BIPAP	Bilevel Positive Airway Pressure
BOQ	Base officer quarters
BOQ	Bachelor Officer Quarters, housing for commissioned officers

BX	Base exchange, similar to a shopping mall
C Company	Charlie Company
C rations	Food rations
C-130	Lockheed C-130 Hercules, troop and cargo transport airplane
CENTCOM	Central Command Commander
CO	Commanding Officer
COBC	Chemical Officer Basic Course
CONUS	Continental United States
CPAP	Continuous Positive Airway Pressure
CSF	Cerebral Spinal Fluid
CT scan	Computerized tomography scan
CUCV	commercial utility cargo vehicle
Deuce and a half	truck that can carry two and half tons
DX	Diagnosis
EDS	Ehlers-Danlos Syndrome
EMT	emergency medical technician
ER	emergency room
FM	field manual
foxhole	hole in the ground used by troops as a shelter or firing point
full bird colonel	full colonel, rank above lieutenant colonel (O-6)
G1	General staff position 1, human resources

GAFPB	German Armed Forces Proficiency Badge
GP	General purpose
guidon	pennant that narrows to a fork at the free end
HI	Hosteling International
HMMWV	Colloquial: Humvee, a High Mobility Multipurpose Wheeled Vehicle
IV	Intravenous therapy
JAG	judge advocate general
KP	Kitchen Police, menial and/or unskilled assistance in the mess hall kitchen
L (the)	The Loop, the elevated transit system in Chicago
land nav	land navigation
LBE	Load bearing equipment
LLL!	Live, Love, Laugh!
LOD	Line of Duty
m-day	First day of mobilization
MEPS	Military Entrance Processing Station
mess hall	a room or building where groups of people eat together
MOB	Main Operating Base
MRE	Meals, Ready-to-Eat
MRI	Magnetic resonance imagery
MTOE	Modification Table of Organization and Equipment, manning roster
MWR	Morale, Welfare, and Recreation

NATO	North Atlantic Treaty Organization
NBCR	Nuclear, Biological, and Chemical or Radiological
NCO	Noncommissioned officer
OBC	Officer Basic Course
OCS	Officer Candidate School, known in 2020 as BOLC or the Basic Officer Leadership Course
OD	Olive drab
OER	Officer Evaluation Report
OJT	On-the-job training
ordnance	artillery/armament maintenance
OSB	Officer Selection Battery
PRC-10	Portable radio communication
PROTRAIN	Provisional Roundout Training
PT	Physical fitness OR Physical Therapy
PTSD	Post-traumatic stress disorder
PX	Post exchange, also known as the BX (base exchange), or NEX (Navy Exchange)
R&R	Repair and replace/ Rest & Relaxation, time off of duty
R2R	Ride2Recovery
ROTC	Reserve Officers' Training Corps
RTO	Radiotelephone Operator
ruck	Rucksack
S4	Staff logistics officer, individual responsible for battalion transportation, supplies, and maintenance

SECDEF	Secretary of Defense
SOAP notes	subjective symptoms, objective signs, assessment or diagnosis, and plan of treatment
SPT BN	support battalion
SSN	Social security number
staff puke	dismissive, disregarding, or derogatory reference to a person, usually of a different unit or branch, used in the same sense of grind or DRONE for a worker or laborer
TAC	Training, Advising, and Counseling
TBI	Traumatic Brain Injury
TDRL	Temporary Disability Retirement List
The Big Red One	1st infantry division, per the shoulder patch insignia
tinys	Slang for GP Small tents, approximately 18' across with 5'8" tall side walls and a 10' foot center height
tour	period of time spent in service
tracers	(or tracer rounds) ammunition with pyrotechnic charge that allows it to be seen once fired
UNOS	United Network for Organ Sharing
USO	United Service Organization
USTRANSCOM	United States Transportation Command
VA	Veterans Affairs/ Veterans Administration
XO	Executive Officer

TIMELINE

1954	Lita is born in Southern Illinois
1960-1968	Lita attends Saint Peter Canisius Catholic School
1968-1972	Lita attends Oak Park River Forest High School
1972	Lita marries Pete
1974	Lita's daughter Jean Marie is born
1975	Lita's daughter Kymberly is born
1977	Lita joins the Army
1977	Lita gets divorced
1978-9	Lita is attached to the Big Red One, 1st Infantry Division, Ft. Riley, KS
1984	Lita transfers to the Air Force
1986	Lita attends OCS
1987	Lita's OBC, Aberdeen Proving Grounds, MD
1989-1992	Jean attends Riverside Brookfield High School
1990	Lita's marriage to Anton Tomas
1993	Lita joins the ILARNG, 108th Support Battalion, staff, North Riverside, IL
1994	Jean's Basic Training, Ft. Jackson, SC
1994	Jean's Advanced Individual Training, Ft. Sam Houston, TX
1997	Lita holds company command, B Co, 108th Support BN
1998-9	Jean attends OCS
1999-2000	Jean's OBC, Ft. Leonard Wood, MO
2002-2004	Lita is on Active Duty, Joint Command, Scott AFB
2004	Lita retires from the military

2004 Jean has brain surgery, decompression, and laminectomy, University of Chicago

2005 Jean's shoulder blade surgery, resection, University of Chicago

2007 Jean's shoulder blade surgery, muscle reattachment, Lexington, KY

2007 Jean receives a medical discharge from the military

2011 Jean's repeated falls, syncopies, and fractured cribriform plate

2012 Jean's brainstem impingement, cranial cervical fusion, Great Neck, NY

2013 Professional Responsibility Review Board of Archdiocese of Chicago conducts their Second Stage Review and unanimously determines there is reasonable cause to suspect that Peter John McNamara engaged in acts of sexual misconduct with a minor (Lita).

2015 Jean's ankle surgery

2017 Cousin's liver transplant, Duke University Hospital, Durham, NC

2018 Lita, Jean, & their friend Ron start PodcastDX, an interview based podcast that allow real patients to tell their diagnosis story

2020 PodcastDX nominated for Wego Health Award: Best in Show Podcast for the third year in a row

2020 PodcastDX nominated for the Ambies: Best Interview Podcast

INDEX

CPSIA information can be obtained
at www.ICGtesting.com
Printed in the USA
LVHW081405100222
710636LV00002B/4/J